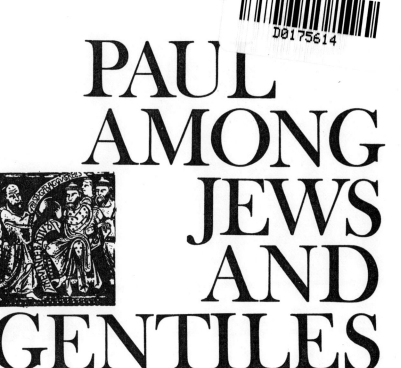

PAUL AMONG JEWS AND GENTILES

AND OTHER ESSAYS

Krister Stendahl

Fortress Press

Philadelphia

The essay, "Paul Among Jews and Gentiles," is based on
the Thomas White Currie Lectures delivered at the Austin
Presbyterian Seminary, February 4–8, 1963, and on the Ayer
Lectures delivered at the Colgate Rochester Divinity School,
March 30–April 1, 1964.

Cover art detail from:
Paul in Dispute with Jews and Gentiles

Biblical quotations when taken from the Revised Standard
Version of the Bible, copyright 1946, 1952, © 1971, 1973
by the Division of Christian Education of the National Council of the Churches of Christ in the U.S.A., are used by
permission.

Fourth printing 1980

———————

Library of Congress Catalog Card Number 75-36450
ISBN 0-8006-1224-8

———————

8959K80   Printed in the United States of America   1-1224

See Geo. Foote Moore

CONTENTS

Preface   v

Paul Among Jews and Gentiles   1
     1   Paul Among Jews and Gentiles   1
     2   Call Rather Than Conversion   7
     3   Justification Rather
           Than Forgiveness   23
     4   Weakness Rather Than Sin   40
     5   Love Rather Than Integrity   52
     6   Unique Rather Than Universal   67

The Apostle Paul and the Introspective
     Conscience of the West   78

Judgment and Mercy   97

Glossolalia—The New Testament Evidence   109

Sources and Critiques   125

To the memory of
Emilie T. Sander
my scholar-friend
without whose encouragement
and devoted work this book
would not have seen the light of day.

PREFACE

Some years ago I gave the Thomas White Currie Lectures at the Austin Presbyterian Theological Seminary. At that time I took certain steps toward an interpretation of Paul which grew out of an article long in the making and finally entitled, "The Apostle Paul and the Introspective Conscience of the West" (included as the second essay in this book, p. 78, below), an English revision in 1961 of an article published in Sweden in 1960. Since then I have often returned to the themes and ideas in the Currie Lectures of 1963, and elaborated on further in the Ayer Lectures at the Colgate Rochester Divinity School in 1964. I have subsequently often considered various shifts and angles and I have wanted to give them adequate thought as they increasingly became very important to me. They could not be brushed aside as whimsical hunches. Over the past fifteen years I have tried out my ideas in different milieus, lands and languages, in academic settings, in church groups, among clergy, and with lay people.

Now the time has come for me to recognize that whatever insights I may have they are perhaps most useful to others if I share them more or less in the impressionistic form of the lecture style. As a scholar I recognize the vulnerability of these lectures, but it could also be that one virtue of the popular lecture style is that it allows your colleagues and critics to see what you think when you cannot balance every statement by cautionary protection, be it with footnotes or by the guarded precision of noncommitment. I am grateful to Fortress Press for encouraging me to proceed, and to Norman Hjelm and Ingalill Hellman Hjelm for their assistance beyond the calls of duty.

I must confess that today I would at some point say things a little differently, but on the whole my research and reflection over the intervening years have corroborated the perspective which I originally tried to communicate in those lectures.

The most important shift in my position centers in my more recent understanding of Paul's Epistle to the Romans. When I gave these lectures I was heavily under the spell of Johannes Munck's studies of Paul. During his long periods of research at Uppsala University he became the one who opened up the Pauline world to me—as we both felt the refreshing impact of Anton Fridrichsen's *The Apostle and His Message* (1947). As Fridrichsen was my exegetical father, so Munck became my older brother. As my life of teaching and preaching continued I arrived at a critical distance from them both—and I never quite understood what led Munck into his labored defense of an early date for the Book of Acts and of its utterly dependable nature. But this is a good place to express my gratitude to both Fridrichsen and Munck for the exciting paths which they cleared for me which opened new vistas which they in some ways viewed differently than I.

Munck's interpretation of Paul's apostolic ministry as ultimately aimed at the salvation of Israel now strikes me as a tour de force. In the first section of the present essay on "Paul Among Jews and Gentiles" I hope to tell why, and suggest a different model that I find more compelling. But when these lectures were originally conceived and given I shared Munck's view.

The lectures are also somewhat dated in other ways. I am conscious of how blessed we are by the way in which our sisters (in and outside the movement) have unmasked the sexist character of our linguistic habits. I have not attempted a consistent "de-sexing" of the language. I believe that requires original thinking from a less sexist perspective than I had in those days, more than an editorial task. Thus, for example, this text is rich in the generic use of "man." I let it stand as a witness to where I was. Such a witness is the more embarrassing to me since I was deeply concerned about the Bible and the role of women long before these lectures were given.

The biblical quotations in these lectures are from the RSV, except at points where I find special reason to translate otherwise. In the lectures—which were delivered from notes and were taped—I translated from the Greek as I went along, or quoted from memory, often inaccurately in respect to elements of little importance for my argument.

I have been greatly, I would say, indispensably assisted in all of this by my long-time collaborator Dr. Emilie T. Sander. Her preparation of these lectures for publication was her last work. Two weeks after sending the manuscript to Fortress Press she died in her sleep on June 4, 1976, struck by a massive heart attack. In dedicating this book to her memory I wish to express in a small way my gratitude for her encouragement and her unselfish work in helping to transfer my thoughts and observations from the spoken to the printed word, and from the Swedish to the English language. Our collaboration reached back to her days at Union Seminary in New York in the late 1950's where she was my teaching assistant in the summer school. She translated and edited the American edition of my book, *The Bible and the Role of Women.* On the basis of her lecture notes from my various courses at Harvard she prepared the basic text for our contribution on "Biblical Literature" to the 1975 edition of the *Encyclopaedia Britannica,* a project which would never have been completed had she not taken on a larger share of the work than the designation of co-authorship, K. St./E. T. Sa., suggests to the reader. Concerning the essay on "Paul Among Jews and Gentiles," again, I would not have been able to arrive at publication without her energetic and intelligent devotion to the task.

Emilie Sander was an unusually intelligent and perceptive scholar. My gratitude to her is coupled with the painful question whether I profited so much from her work that this deprived us all from hearing more from her speaking, writing, thinking in her own idiom, and from her own perceptions.

Dr. Sander labored valiantly on the present manuscript in order to find a reasonable middle-ground between the overly talkative carelessness of taped transcriptions and formal written style. She tried to produce a book that would fit the intention of serious, yet non-technical communication. She knew me well, and she often had to point out to me that one cannot transcribe the tone or the smile that alerts the audience to what is said in jest or with irony. Yet, we tried together to find that balance.

It is my conviction that theology is too serious to allow humans to think theologically without playfulness and irony. To try to be as serious as the subject would be arrogant, and could lead the hearer/reader to believe that I considered everything to be precisely as I describe it. Of late I have become even more convinced of the theological necessity of irony—and of its nobler cousin humor—as a safeguard against idolatry. I believe that to be a reason why Jesus chose to speak in parables, most of which have a humorous twist. And the Jewish tradition, rabbinic, hasidic, and contemporary, is marked by a persistent cultivation of the telling of stories with a humorous slant—a point often missed by "serious" theologians. In this area I have learned a lot from Brita, my wife, in her work on Kierkegaard, whose famous melancholy should not overshadow his irony and humor.

Theology of the kind I am doing in this book has a playful, tentative character. For, as Paul said, knowledge—even prophecy—is imperfect. If one forgets that, it "puffs up" (1 Cor. 8:1). And I like to think as a child, reason as a child, for as a Christian I have not yet grown up, or relinquished my childish ways. That would be wrong before the day comes when by God's grace we shall understand fully, even as we will be fully understood (1 Cor. 13:8–13). In the meantime I invite other children to come and play with me.

The works of the late Johannes Munck, to which I refer in this Preface, are: *Paul and the Salvation of Mankind* (Richmond: John Knox Press, 1959; German original, 1954). This work remains a masterpiece and one sadly overlooked in Pauline scholarship. It was followed in 1956 by *Christ and Israel. An Interpretation of Romans 9–11* (Philadelphia: Fortress Press, 1967) to which I wrote the foreword. Munck's commentary to the Books of Acts was published posthumously and revised by W. F. Albright and C. S. Mann in *The Anchor Bible*, Vol. 31 (New York: Doubleday, 1967).

For Kierkegaard on irony and humor, I refer to Brita K. Stendahl, *Søren Kierkegaard*, published in the Twayne *World Author Series* 392 (Boston: Twayne Publishers, 1976), especially, the section in "The Concept of Irony," pp. 36–45.

1 Paul Among Jews and Gentiles

Paul lived his life among Jews and Gentiles. That is not a surprising or particularly controversial statement. As a Jew he had grown accustomed to dividing humankind into those two parts. In some of his letters the very structure of his argument is itself accounted for by that dichotomy. Often, moreover, his reference to "all" is synonymous with "both Jews and Greeks." According to his own words he is the Apostle to the Gentiles; in writing to Rome, he speaks of his obligation to both Greeks and barbarians, yet in fulfilling that obligation he is much aware of the Jews and their role in God's plan (Romans 1:14–16). In Acts Paul is programmatically portrayed as the Jew, the ex-Pharisee who brings the gospel to the Gentile world and that book does not end until Paul has made it all the way to Rome, the seat of power in the Gentile world.

On further reflection, however, the title of this book and this essay—*Paul Among Jews and Gentiles*—is not quite as innocent or bland as it may appear. It will be my contention in these chapters that the main lines of Pauline interpretation —and hence both conscious and unconscious reading and quoting of Paul by scholars and lay people alike—have for many centuries been out of touch with one of the most basic of the questions and concerns that shaped Paul's thinking in the first place: the relation between Jews and Gentiles.

Especially in the Protestant tradition—and particularly among Lutherans—it is Paul's Epistle to the Romans which holds a position of honor, supplying patterns of thought that are lifted into the position of overarching and organizing principles for the Pauline material. Paul's presentation of justification by faith has such a role; to some this serves not only as the key to Pauline thought, but as the criterion for the really true gospel as it is to be found in the whole New Testament, the whole Bible, and the long and varied history of Christian theology.

The following chapters will demonstrate how such a doctrine of justification by faith was hammered out by Paul for the very specific and limited purpose of defending the rights of Gentile converts to be full and genuine heirs to the promises of God to Israel. Their rights were based solely on faith in Jesus Christ. This was Paul's very special stance, and he defended it zealously against any compromise that required circumcision or the keeping of kosher food laws by Gentile Christians. As the Apostle to the Gentiles he defended this view as part and parcel of the special assignment and revelation that he had received directly from God. In none of his writings does he give us information about what he thought to be proper in these matters for Jewish Christians. Himself a Jew, but with a special mission to the Gentiles, Paul is never heard to urge Jewish Christians to live like him in these respects. When he admonishes parishioners to imitate him he seems always to refer to himself not using his privilege or freedom to the full (1 Cor. 11:1; Phil. 3:17). When he rebukes Peter in Antioch, it is not for Peter's practice of keeping a kosher table but for Peter's changing his attitudes under pressure from Jerusalem (Gal. 2:11ff). For as Paul says in Romans, "Let everyone act with full conviction" (14:5), and "for all that is not out of conviction is sin" (14:23). In respect to his defense of the rights and the freedom of *Gentile* converts, Paul has provided ample and full documentation in Galatians, a letter to which we shall return.

All this does not sound much different from what we are used to hearing. How or why then do I claim that in our traditional understanding we have lost touch with the image of Paul among Jews and Gentiles? For one simple reason;

while Paul addresses himself to the relation of Jews to Gentiles, we tend to read him as if his question was: On what
grounds, on what terms, are we to be saved? We think that
Paul spoke about justification by faith, using the Jewish-Gentile
situation as an instance, as an example. But Paul was chiefly
concerned about the relation between Jews and Gentiles—and
in the development of *this* concern he used as one of his arguments the idea of justification by faith.

Such a shift in focus and perception blocks our access both
to the original thought and the original intention of Paul. It
leads to distortions of our historical description of Paul's ministry and to misunderstandings of Paul as a person. It leads
to a misconstruction of the problem Paul intended to solve by
his observations on faith and law and salvation. The fact of
the matter is that if we read Paul's answer to the question of
how Gentiles become heirs to God's promises to Israel as if
he were responding to Luther's pangs of conscience, it becomes
obvious that we are taking the Pauline answer out of its
original context.

The lost centrality of "Jews and Gentiles" is most clearly
to be felt in a study of Romans. What is Romans about?
Why did Paul write this letter at that crucial point in his
career when he was through with the East, had gathered the
collection for the Jerusalem church (cf. Gal. 2:10), and was
delivering it prior to setting out for the West via Rome? My
guess is that it was not his purpose to write a theological
tractate on the nature of justification by faith. No. Here is
rather the Apostle Paul among Jews and Gentiles, introducing
his mission to the significant, but to him unknown, church in
Rome. He wants to make clear to them how his mission fits
into God's total plan and scheme. It is of more than passing
interest to note how this letter differs from that to the Galatians. There the discussion was about *Judaizers*, i.e. Gentiles
infatuated with Jewish ways. In Romans, on the other hand,
Paul speaks about *Jews*.

This is not the place for an extensive analysis of Romans,
but it may be helpful to remember how Paul's *apologia*, his

presentation of his mission, becomes a panoramic view of how his Gentile mission fits into God's total plan, and how that perspective finally brings him to the point where he sees that Christianity is on its way to becoming a Gentile church. Simultaneously he sees that God has mysterious and special plans for the salvation of Israel. This, the mystery of Israel's separate existence, Paul proclaims to the Gentiles "lest you be conceited" (Rom. 11:25) in an uncalled-for feeling of superiority.

To me the climax of Romans is actually chapters 9—11, i.e., his reflections on the relation between church and synagogue, the church and the Jewish *people*—not "Christianity" and "Judaism," not the attitudes of the gospel versus the attitudes of the law. The question is the relation between two communities and their coexistence in the mysterious plan of God.

It should be noted that Paul does not say that when the time of God's kingdom, the consummation, comes Israel will accept Jesus as the Messiah. He says only that the time will come when "all Israel will be saved" (11:26). It is stunning to note that Paul writes this whole section of Romans (10:18–11:36) without using the name of Jesus Christ. This includes the final doxology (11:33–36), the only such doxology in his writings without any christological element.

Such random observations about Romans make it quite clear that in this letter Paul's focus really is the relation between Jews and Gentiles, not the notion of justification or predestination and certainly not other proper yet abstract theological topics.

It is tempting to suggest that in important respects Paul's thought here approximates an idea well documented in later Jewish thought from Maimonides to Franz Rosenzweig. Christianity—and in the case of Maimonides, also Islam—is seen as the conduit of Torah, for the declaration of both monotheism and the moral order to the Gentiles. The differences are obvious, but the similarity should not be missed: Paul's reference to God's mysterious plan is an affirmation of a God-willed coexistence between Judaism and Christianity in which the missionary urge to convert Israel is held in check.

It goes without saying that Paul's primary focus on Jews and Gentiles was lost in the history of interpretation, and when it was retained, the church picked up the negative side of the "mystery"—Israel's "No" to Jesus Christ—but totally missed the warning against conceit and feelings of superiority. Once this mystery became inoperative in the central thinking of the church, the Jews being written off as God-killers and as stereotypes for wrong attitudes toward God, the road was ever more open for beautiful spiritualizations of Pauline theology. Romans became a theological tractate on the nature of faith. Justification no longer "justified" the status of Gentile Christians as honorary Jews, but became the timeless answer to the plights and pains of the introspective conscience of the West. And Paul was no longer seen "among Jews and Gentiles" but rather as the guide for those perplexed and troubled by the human predicament. His teaching was now detached from what he had seen as his task, his mission, and his aim—to be the Apostle to the Gentiles.

Once the human predicament—timeless and exercised in a *corpus christianum*—became the setting of the church's interpretation of Paul's thought, it also became less obvious that there was in fact a great difference of setting, thought, and argument between the various epistles of Paul. As his teaching of justification was removed from its setting within the relationship between Jew and Gentile and became part of his teaching about salvation, the difference between Jews in Romans and Judaizers in Galatians also came to have little interest. Further, it became difficult and irrelevant to notice that the Corinthian or the Thessalonian correspondence had a yet totally different vocabulary, problematic and intention. It was possible to homogenize Pauline theology since the common denominator could easily be found in generalized theological issues, and the specificity of Paul's arguments was obscured. In 1 Corinthians, however, we have a fascinating window into "Paul among the Gentiles." In the chapters that follow we shall note with some precision how rich and varied Paul's thinking is, and how such awareness requires attention to the setting as to Jews and Gentiles.

Yet the question arises: How can letters which Paul directed to specific churches in specific situations be the word of God for the church at large and in all times? It is intriguing to recall that one of the earliest discussions that has survived, that of the Canon Muratori, a Latin list of the New Testament books deemed to be in the canon (usually dated in the second century, but recently placed in the fourth by Albert Sundberg), recognizes the problem involved in designating letters written to individual congregations as the word of God for all. Its solution is ingenious. In the Muratorian Canon it is noted that Paul addressed seven churches, and in the Revelation of John seven churches are addressed (chs. 1—3) as if addressing the church at large. It seems to follow that we can accept Paul's epistles as Scripture, on the basis of an analogy to the seven churches in the Book of Revelation. This is obviously a subsequent rationalization, but it explains how the mind of the church in Rome tried to explain to itself what was already a fact—that the collection of Pauline epistles was included in the canon. In a way the number seven was seen as being in conscious conformity to the pattern of God's own revelation in the Johannine Apocalypse, *ergo* Paul's letters are intended for the whole church, having a catholic (general) intention.

But once the individual letters were acknowledged as Scripture they quickly suffered homogenization. In the last section of this essay we shall have reason to reflect further on the value of keeping these letters distinct, at least for the purpose of making sure what questions the Apostle intended to answer. Even the divinely right answer is not heard aright if it is applied to the wrong question.

In what follows I have taken the risk of coining some slogan-like titles by which I hope to unmask Paul's original intentions. When I speak in this adversative form—"Justification rather than Forgiveness," "Weakness rather than Sin," or "Call rather than Conversion," etc.—I am not suggesting that Paul explicitly or implicitly was against, say, forgiveness. I am only using the word-study approach in a quite elementary fashion which is available to any Bible reader. And I use it for the purpose of showing how some of the things that we often seem to hear and perceive in Paul either are not there or are there for a very different reason or purpose than we assume. That is all. Thus I have used a method which is far from esoteric. My hope is that readers of the Bible will be able not only to follow the argument, but to take it and continue on their own. Our vision is often more obstructed by ✓ what we think we know than by our lack of knowledge. It is with that conviction that this book will be short on erudition and dogged in its insistence on a simple reading of the text.

2 Call Rather Than Conversion

Paul's experience on the Damascus Road is usually referred to as his Conversion. In Acts there are three accounts of this episode (9:1–19; 22:4–16; 26:9–19), and there is material in Paul's own Epistle to the Galatians (1:11–17). From reading these accounts it seems reasonable to speak of the event as a "conversion" since that is our usual term for such an occurrence. It appears that a Jew, so strong in his Jewish faith that he persecutes Christians, himself becomes a Christian through a sudden and overwhelming experience. Yet a closer reading of these accounts, both those in Acts and those by Paul himself, reveals a greater continuity between "before" and "after." Here is not that change of "religion" that we commonly associate with the word *conversion*. Serving the one and the same God, Paul receives a new and special calling in God's service. God's Messiah asks him as a Jew to bring God's message to the Gentiles. The emphasis in the accounts is always on this assignment, not on the conversion. Rather than being "converted," Paul was called to the specific task—made clear to him by his experience of the risen Lord—of apostleship to the Gentiles, one hand-picked through Jesus Christ on behalf of the one God of Jews and Gentiles.

On the assumption that what a man reveals about himself

is on the whole more accurate than what is recounted by others,
let us first examine Paul's own account of his call to this particular mission. After Paul says that he received the gospel
through a revelation of Jesus Christ (Gal. 1:12), he adds:
"For you heard of my former life in Judaism, how I persecuted the church of God violently and tried to destroy it; and
I advanced in Judaism beyond many of my own age among
my people, so extremely zealous was I for the traditions of
my fathers. But when he who had set me apart before I was
born, and had called me through his grace, was pleased to
reveal his Son to me, in order that I might preach him among
the Gentiles . . ." (Gal. 1:13–16). This is the most explicit
reference made by Paul about what we are accustomed to refer
to as his conversion. If this passage is read in the standard
edition of the Greek text (Nestle-Aland) one notes certain
indications that Paul has alluded to Old Testament passages in
this account. Most English translations with footnotes or
cross references also make this clear. Paul says that God has
set him apart from his mother's womb, called him through
grace, and given him a mission to the Gentiles. The prophet
Isaiah writes, "The Lord called me from the womb, from the
body of my mother he named my name" (Isa. 49:1), and
"I will give you as a light to the nations, that my salvation may
reach to the ends of the earth" (Isa. 49:6). The call of the
prophet Jeremiah is similar, "Before I formed you in the womb
I knew you, and before you were born I consecrated you; I
appointed you a prophet to the nations" i.e. the Gentiles,
goyim (Jer. 1:5). Thus in Galatians Paul describes his experience in terms of a prophetic call similar to that of Isaiah and
Jeremiah. He felt hand-picked by God after the prophetic
model to take the message of God and Christ to the Gentiles.
In Philippians, he stresses that he is "a Hebrew born of
Hebrews, as to the law a Pharisee, as to zeal a persecutor of
the church, as to righteousness under the law blameless"
(Phil. 3:5–6). Yet without casting doubts as to the worth
of his background but pointing out that his former values,
great though they were, are as nothing in light of his knowl-

edge and recognition of Christ, he continues, "But whatever gain I had, I counted as loss for the sake of Christ. Indeed I count everything as loss because of the surpassing worth of knowing Christ Jesus my Lord. For his sake I suffered loss of all things and count them as refuse in order that I may gain Christ and be found in him, not having a righteousness of my own, based on law, but that which is faith in Christ, the righteousness of God that depends on faith . . ." (Phil. 3:7–9). It thus becomes clear that the usual conversion model of Paul the Jew who gives up his former faith to become a Christian is not the model of Paul but of ours. Rather, his call brings him to a new understanding of his mission, a new understanding of the law which is otherwise an obstacle to the Gentiles. His ministry is based on the specific conviction that the Gentiles will become part of the people of God without having to pass through the law. This is Paul's secret revelation and knowledge.

Of course Paul's account of his call to apostleship has its own particular and necessarily apologetic slant. There were those, possibly in the Jerusalem church, who would reject his direct apostolic authority and demand that such apostleship must be granted him by higher human authorities. Paul vigorously denies this and asserts his direct calling, "I would have you know, brethren, that the gospel which was preached by me is not man's gospel. For I did not receive it from man, nor was I taught it, but it came from a revelation of Jesus Christ" (Gal. 1:11–12).

In Acts the notion of a "call" is still dominant although more details are given concerning Paul's experience. His call is mediated to him, in Acts 9, by Ananias who is told by the Lord that Paul is a "chosen instrument" (Acts 9:15). Here in Luke's narrative the image of the Lord's chosen agent also recalls Jeremiah 1:5 (cf. 1:10) and Isaiah 49:1. But the event is not seen as conversion from one "religion" to another, but as a call to that specific mission of which Ananias is told, "For the Lord said to him, 'Go, for he is a chosen instrument of mine to carry my name before the Gentiles and kings and the

sons of Israel . . .' " (Acts 9:15). In Acts 22 it is again Ananias who tells Paul, "The God of our fathers appointed you to
know his will, to see the Just One and to hear a voice from his
mouth; for you will be a witness for him to all men of what
you have seen and heard" (Acts 22:14–15). Then Paul in a
trance hears the Lord say, "Depart; for I will send you far
away to the Gentiles" (Acts 22:21). The account in Acts 26
differs somewhat from Acts 9 and 22 in that Paul sees a light
from heaven and hears the voice of the Lord saying, ". . . rise
and stand upon your feet; for I have appeared to you for this
purpose, to appoint you to serve and witness . . . delivering you
from the people and from the Gentiles, to whom I send you to
open their eyes, that they may turn from darkness to light and
from the power of Satan to God, that they may receive forgiveness of sins and a place among those who are sanctified by faith
in me" (Acts 26:16–18). In this passage the vision and call
of the prophet Ezekiel are recalled, virtually a direct reference
to Ezekiel 1:28, in which there is visionary experience, prostra-
tion, and subsequently the voice of the Lord saying, ". . . stand
upon your feet. . . . I send you to the people of Israel, to a
nation of rebels. . . ." (Ezek. 2:1,3). Paul's commission to go
to the Gentiles also recalls Jeremiah, ". . . to all to whom I
send you you shall go, and whatever I command you you shall
speak" (Jer. 1:7). Furthermore, what Paul is to accomplish
for the Gentiles (Acts 26:18) is a reflection of the prophecies
that the eyes of the blind shall be opened (Isa. 35:5; 42:7, 16)
and that salvation will come (Isa. 61:1).

While the accounts in Acts, especially in chapters 9 and 22,
to some extent take the position that Paul had to have his
experience interpreted to him, both Galatians and Acts nevertheless reflect a similar tradition, namely that of a prophetic call.
If, then, we use the term "conversion" for Paul's experience,
we would also have to use it of such prophets as Jeremiah and
Isaiah. Yet we do not speak of their conversion, but rather
of their call. Paul's experience is also that of a call—to a
specific vocation—to be God's appointed Apostle to the Gentiles. The mission is the point. It is a call to mission rather

than a conversion. And this call is the greater since it is the persecutor who becomes the apostle.

We often hear that the change in Paul's life caused by his conversion was so great that he was given a new name: Saul became Paul. But that is not how Acts sees it. Actually, the change of name in Acts is quite instructive in the context of discussing call rather than conversion. To begin with, there are three and not two names in the Greek text: *Saulos* (Saul) through 13:9; and *Paulos* (Paul) from 13:9 on, except for the transliteration of the Hebrew name, *Saoul* in the actual accounts of the call, used both by the Lord and by Ananias (9:4, 17; 22:7, 13; 26:14). Thus it is obviously not the call/conversion that triggers the name change. The crucial editorial seam (13:9) has the following setting: *Saulos* is on Cyprus, competing with a magician, a Jewish prophet, Bar Jesus/Elymas before a Roman proconsul by the name of Sergius Paulus. Then verse 9 reads: "But *Saulos*, who is also called Paulos, filled with the Holy Spirit . . . said . . ." And from that point on the book of Acts calls him Paul. Why? This is Paul's first encounter with Roman officals, and if the purpose of Acts is to show the gospel's way from Jerusalem to Rome (cf. Acts 1:8), then it is clear that the name change symbolizes the change of focus. From now on, Rome is the "magnet". The mission is in focus—therefore the call, not the conversion.

What, then, is the difference between a call and a conversion? Perhaps not too much, but without quibbling, let us focus on the proper distinction between the words. Most of us in the Western tradition have come to think of Paul's development as coterminous with what we commonly describe as a conversion experience. But this leads to two difficulties for a right understanding of Paul. In the first place, the term "conversion" easily causes us to bring into play the idea that Paul "changed his religion": the Jew became a Christian. But there is ample reason to question such a model. To begin with, people in those days did not think about "religions." And, furthermore, it is obvious that Paul remains a Jew as he fulfills his role as an Apostle to the Gentiles.

In the second place, by using the idea of conversion we are apt to separate Paul, a person with a highly specific experience, from the general religious experience of that encounter with Christ which convinces and which creates faith. And since Paul's conversion experience was so deep and of such a quality that it even made him a missionary and apostle, we separate his being Christian from his being an apostle. But the texts (Acts and Paul's own letters) agree in quite another image: the persecutor was called and chosen to be an apostle with a very special mission which focused on how the gospel should reach the Gentiles. Again and again we find that there is hardly a thought of Paul's which is not tied up with his mission, with his work. The "I" in his writings is not "the Christian" but "the Apostle to the Gentiles." That is why I say call rather than conversion.

Here is a point at which it is equally important to discern the differences between Paul and Luther. Paul's experience is not of that inner experience of conversion which Western theology has taken for granted. What is behind this distinction is something very serious. It is that we all, in the West, and especially in the tradition of the Reformation, cannot help reading Paul through the experience of persons like Luther or Calvin. And this is the chief reason for most of our misunderstandings of Paul. In Luther, for example, we have a man who labors under the threatening demands of the law—a man in despair, a man for whom *the* theological and existential question is "How am I to find a gracious God?" He was a person who recognized that the harder he tried, the more he fell short, a person who precisely in his piety reached the very depths of the abyss of futility and shortcomings before God, a person who walked to the very gates of Hell; a person who knew guilt in its most introspective intensity. And this young man Luther found in Paul and in his words on how "the righteous shall live by faith" and in similar sayings, *the* message of God which lifted him out of despair and placed him in that mighty fortress of grace about which he wrote his stirring hymn.

Contrast Paul, a very happy and successful Jew, one who

can, even when he thinks about it from his Christian perspective, say in his Epistle to the Philippians ". . . as to the righteousness under the law (I was) blameless" (Phil. 3:6). That *is* what he says. He experiences no troubles, no problems, no qualms of conscience, no feelings of shortcomings. He is a star pupil, the student to get the thousand dollar graduate scholarship in Gamaliel's Seminary, if we can trust Acts (22:3) —both for character and for achievements of scholarship—a very happy Jew. Nowhere in Paul's writings is there any indication that he had any difficulties in fulfilling what he as a Jew understood to be the requirements of the law. We often quote and preach wonderful sermons about the words of Paul, ". . . forgetting what lies behind and straining forward to what lies ahead, I press on . . ." (Phil. 3:13ff). But few are those who can read their Bibles with sufficient simplicity as to understand what it is that Paul forgets: his achievements, not his shortcomings. It is all those achievements which he now says appear like rubbish (Phil. 3:8). There is no indication that psychologically Paul had some problem of conscience with which he *had* had, or was to have any major difficulties. As a Jew he had never been down in the Valley of Despond. He went from glory unto glory. The fact that past glories led him to become a persecutor of the church caused him some remorse *after* his call (1 Cor. 15:9), but there is no indication of such remorse or doubts prior to his call to the mission. In the three accounts in Acts we are also struck by the lack of any note of incrimination or self-incrimination when Paul the persecutor is mentioned. That the persecutor became the Apostle makes only for more glory to God.

These accounts strike me as quite different from the "tower experience" of Luther, and from the whole tradition of the Reformation. And especially is this so in the latest existentially psychologized stages of that tradition marked by the attempts of us Christian preachers to outdo the psychologists, not to say the psychiatrists, in our morbid and masochistic ability to describe the futility and the shortcomings of all human attempts and hopes.

But does not Paul ever speak of himself as a sinner? He certainly does. But the only concrete sin *qua* sin in his life, *the* sin which he mentions, is that he had persecuted the church (1 Cor. 15:9). To recognize that kind of sin does not require an introspective conscience. And he also says, quite frankly, that he has made up for that sin and, moreover, he is proud of the extent to which he has made up for it: "... I have worked harder than any of them (the other apostles)..." (1 Cor. 15:10) who had not committed that awful sin. Of course, it was not he who accomplished this: "It was not I, but the grace of God which is with me" (1 Cor. 15:10). Paul is confident that he has made up for the only sin which he speaks about concretely. Here is a man with a quite robust conscience. Here is a man not plagued by introspection. The difference between Paul and Luther and, perhaps, modern Western man, is precisely at that point. It certainly sounds strange to us when in 2 Corinthians 5:10–11 Paul demonstrates his good conscience before the church: "For we all must appear before the judgment seat of Christ, so that each one may receive good or evil, according to what he has done ..." And he goes on to tell the Corinthians that even in the presence of that judgment and with that fear of God before his eyes, he has been cleared (2 Cor. 5:11). Then he adds that he hopes that they have as favorable an impression of him. That does not sound very modest. That does not sound like a man who is conscious of the fact that he is at the same time justified and sinner, *simul justus et peccator.* So something seems askew in our reading if we think that Paul was troubled by sin.

It is important to sharpen these perceptions as we look at Paul's own letters. We have already pointed to two factors which may explain our sense of strangeness in this confrontation. Primarily it is our own Western introspective thinking that leads us astray. But then we ask: Is Paul speaking about his "clean conscience" (1 Cor. 4) as a missionary rather than as a private citizen? Or is it, rather, that Paul, the Christian, is just as sure of himself as Paul, the Jew—or vice versa? I think that his conscience seems robust. This is surely reflected in 1 Corinthians 4:1–5:

> This is how one should regard us, as servants of Christ and stewards of the mysteries of God. Moreover it is required of stewards that they be found trustworthy. But with me it is a very small thing that I should be judged by you or by any human court. I do not even judge myself, but I have not been justified by this, but it is the Lord who judges me. Therefore do not pronounce judgment before the time, before the Lord comes, who will bring to light the things now hidden in darkness and will disclose the purposes of the heart. Then every man will receive his commendation from God.

Here he pleads for time—even as he occupies the position of the underdog.

What we are touching upon here is one of the most complicated issues of biblical interpretation, the study of Scripture and the Christian life: that it is perhaps not totally true, as we sometimes say, that man is the same through the ages. Usually we allow all sorts of odd sayings to be applied to any situation in any time. The issue, of course, is what is meant by man being "the same." We usually say, "basically the same" or "essentially the same." That is, of course, the safety catch which lets the truth evaporate or be attenuated or changed according to varying situations. It is quite clear that in the very basic understanding of man's predicament there is a gulf not only between Paul and us, but between the New Testament and our time. We must somehow recognize in this chapter that Paul's message was related not to some conversion from the hopeless work righteousness of Judaism into a happy justified status as a Christian. Rather, the center of gravity in Paul's theological work is related to the fact that he knew himself to be called to be the Apostle to the Gentiles, an Apostle of the one God who is Creator of both Jews and Gentiles (cf. Rom. 3:30).

All this follows from that rather sophisticated distinction between a "call" and a "conversion", a distinction related to one of the classical problems of Pauline studies. Scholars of the West are shocked to find that for at least three hundred years after its writing and distribution the basic insight of Paul's theology—justification by faith (alone), without the works of the law—seems to have been more or less lost in the teaching and thinking of the church. Paul was certainly quoted —after all, he was an apostle, and he was accepted by the church in the canon of sacred Scripture. He was cited with veneration, but as a sort of collection of "golden sayings" which can be found in any decent religious literature. Seldom if ever, however, do we find anyone who had grasped Paul's doctrine of justification.

It was not until Augustine, more than three hundred years after Paul, that a man was found who seemed to see, so to say, what made Paul "tick", and who discerned the center of gravity in Pauline theology: justification. Now the reason for this strange state of affairs is that the early church seems to have felt that Paul spoke about what he actually spoke about, i.e. the relationship between Jews and Gentiles—and that was no problem during those centuries. There was no communication, no ongoing debate of any serious and open kind that touched upon the matter of Jews and Gentiles, and hence Paul's sayings were, in a way, irrelevant. This was rather the time when the very perspective from which Paul saw this relationship was swallowed up in self-serving Christian anti-Judaism, if not anti-Semitism—i.e., the victory of the very attitude which Paul began to detect and combat in the eleventh chapter of Romans.

Augustine, who has perhaps rightly been called the first truly Western man, was the first person in Antiquity or in Christianity to write something so self-centered as his own spiritual autobiography, his *Confessions*. It was he who applied Paul's doctrine of justification to the problem of the introspective conscience, to the question: "On what basis does a person find salvation?" And with Augustine, Western Christianity with its stress on introspective achievements started. It developed in the Middle Ages—with penitential practice and guidance for self-examination coming increasingly to characterize both monastic and secular life—and man became more and more clever in analyzing his ego. Man turned in on himself, infatuated and absorbed by the question not of when God will send deliverance in the history of salvation, but how God is working in the innermost individual soul. The Black Plague, the Black Death, added pressure, and in the piety of the late Middle Ages there were many honest souls. We should not picture this piety only as running around shopping for indulgences and becoming ever more superficial. There were those who took the Word seriously, and they suffered. And one of those who suffered most was Martin Luther, who—not by accident—was an Augustinian. In the grapplings of his introspective conscience, he picked up Paul and found in him God's answer to his problem, the problem of the West, and the problem of the late medieval piety of the West. It is instructive that homiletical material and works on edification from the Greek Church, the Russian Orthodox Church, the Syriac Church, the Coptic Church, the Mar Thoma Church—all of which read their Bibles faithfully, some in languages close to the original tongues of Jesus or of the early versions—contain little of this interest. The introspective conscience is a Western development and a Western plague. Once the introspective conscience came into the theological bloodstream of Western culture, it tended to dominate the scene far beyond its original function. It reached its theological climax and explosion in the Reformation, and its secular climax and explosion in Sigmund Freud. But Paul himself was never involved in this pursuit.

A classic example of the use or, indeed, misuse of Paul may be seen in a comparison of two English translations of Galatians 3:24—both quite permissible from the Greek, yet one obviously biased theologically, and hence for years uncontested since it could be well used in the service of the problem of the introspective conscience. The King James Version of Galatians 3:24 reads, ". . . the law was our schoolmaster to bring us unto Christ . . ." This translation renders the Greek *paidagōgos* as "schoolmaster" (often quoted as "tutor"), and

uses *eis* (*Christon*) as a spatial preposition, "unto." Theologically this is a very useful way of demonstrating that the law
inducing guilt by its fierce commands makes one seek the grace
and forgiveness of new life by coming to Christ. Yet the same
Greek can be translated in a different way and, indeed, more
accurately in terms of the use of *paidagōgos* in and before
Paul's time. Thus the Revised Standard Version reads,
". . . the law was our custodian until Christ came . . ." The
word *paidagōgos* did not mean schoolmaster, tutor or teacher
but rather a "slave" or "strict custodian" who protected a child
on the way to school to see that he came to no harm and was
not molested. And *eis Christon* could be translated temporally,
i.e., until Christ came. Thus, although the Greek allows for
both, the translations reflect very different theological stances.
It is also to be noted that in the King James Version *our*
custodian seems to imply Paul and all the Galatian Christians,
while the RSV clearly intends *our* to apply to Paul and
his fellow Jews. Thus, we have two radically, drastically, and
absolutely opposed understandings of the same Greek phrase,
and the RSV is doubtlessly right both on the basis of the older
meaning of the Greek and on the basis of the context of the
passage (see especially verse 23 with reference to "before").

Now let us examine this passage in its whole context because
it bears precisely on the issue at hand. The context is the situation in Galatia, concern over the question whether Gentiles
could join the church without first being circumcized. Circumcision is at the center of the discussion (2:3; 5:2; 5:11; 6:2).
Paul's argument is that one does not need to go through Judaism into Christianity, but that there is a straight and direct
way to Christ for the Gentiles apart from the law. So far I
think Paul's argument is a familiar one. Perhaps the issue also
dealt with dietary laws, but it came to its climax in the matter
of circumcision. And this is very important. We must constantly look for what Paul is *really* discussing, because whenever we hear about Jews or Judaism or law or circumcision or
dietary laws or feast days or calendars, we say, "Oh, he is
dealing with the problem of legalism." But it is very clear

that Paul solves the problem of circumcision in a much more radical way than in his treatment of the problem of dietary laws. The circumcision of Gentiles is under no circumstances to be accepted. In regard to food laws, however, if the weaker brethren must have some restrictions in order not to stumble, the issue should not be pushed too far. And if we, in our Protestant mood, simply see all these issues as examples of legalism in a general sense, we just do not get the message. This, indeed, might be the reason why we differ so much in Christendom when we face the matter of legalism.

In order to make his point clear Paul must say something about the law. He does so from the perspective of traditional Jewish thought as it was known to him. In that strand of Jewish teaching the law was eternal at both ends, it existed prior to creation and was to last for eternity.

In this passage in Galatians Paul seems to take special pains in proving from the law (quoting only the Pentateuch) that this view is incorrect. Torah for Paul means both the Pentateuch, the first five books of Moses in the Old Testament, and also the law in a more general sense. It is instructive to note that in Galatians 3 and 4 almost all the scriptural passages on which he bases his arguments against the eternal validity of the Torah are taken from the Pentateuch itself. Paul is proving *with* the law something about the law. He is proving with the Torah something *about* the Torah. And what is he saying? He is saying that the law came in 430 years after the promise to Abraham, so it is quite clear that the Torah is not eternal. First came the promise to Abraham and his seed—and Paul held that this "seed" refers to the Christ who was to come. The thrust of Paul's argument is that the law came 430 years after the promise and that that promise was given when the testament or covenant with Abraham was irrevocably signed. Thus the promise stands and the law was added later.

Paul follows this in Galatians 3:19 by enumerating a great many points which belittle the law. First, it was added for transgression's sake. While there is discussion about this, I am quite convinced that it refers to what was a common teaching in both Judaism and in Christianity: that the law received on Sinai was actually a second and revised edition because of what had happened when the first tablets were brought down—they were smashed by Moses in anger because of the golden calf. So Moses went up again to the mountain top to receive a second edition of the law which, say the exegetes, was actually a law which took into account the transgressions of the faithless and disobedient people. And hence this was not the real, pure, ultimate law, but rather a law which was, as all our laws are, tainted by the evil reality it had to counteract. Something like this is probably what is meant when Paul says that the law was added for transgression's sake.

Secondly, the law was given with a time limit—until the coming of the seed ("till the offspring should come to whom the promise had been made," RSV). Thus it is not eternal at the future end either.

Thirdly, "it was ordained by angels through an intermediary." It was communicated by angels—so there had been middlemen. This was usually a point which in the Jewish tradition glorified the law, but Paul turned it the other way around. He even pursues the matter by saying that there was not only one set of middlemen; there was also another middleman, Moses. Thus the law was given not without mediation but through mediators, and, "Now an intermediary implies more than one; but God is one" (Gal. 3:20). By this argument it is not so strange that this law is seen as something other than the ultimate, absolute and immediate manifestation of the salvation of God.

Further, this law was not given in order to give life, for "then righteousness would indeed be by the law" (Gal. 3:21). If a law had been given which would give life, then of course we would be justified by the law. But that is not what the law came for, according to Paul's argument. What did the law come for? Paul says, "the scriptures consigned all things to sin, that what was promised to faith in Jesus Christ might be given to those who believe" (Gal. 3:22). The law came, says Paul, as a harsh baby sitter to see to it that the children of

Israel did not raid the refrigerator before the great party at which the Gentiles should also be present. Or to speak in more biblical language, "Now before faith came, we (Jews) were confined under the law, kept under restraint until faith should be revealed" (Gal. 3:23). In other words, Scripture put everything under lock and key—under sin—in order that the promise should depend on faith in Jesus, the Messiah, and should be given to those who believe in Jesus Christ.

The expressions "until faith should be revealed" (3:23) and "but now that faith has come" (3:25) show an interesting use of the word "faith." We could just as well read "Christ," i.e., "until Christ should be revealed" or "until Christ has come." We are thus led to say that "faith" in the New Testament is not merely a theological attitude; faith is not just having our minds turned toward God and grasping his promises. Faith is totally defined by its content, and when we read "until faith should be revealed" it means until the coming of that Messiah in whom one could believe. But one could not believe in him before he came, because, for Paul, to believe means to accept the messianic claim of Jesus. So before that became possible, which to Paul occurred with the resurrected Lord, the Jews were shut up under the law, "kept under restraint until faith (Christ) should be revealed." Thus the law was our (i.e., Paul's and his fellow Jews') *paidagōgos* until Christ came.

As we have already noted, a "pedagogue" for us is a super-teacher, but in ancient Greek and to Paul it was a person less than a teacher. In ancient Greece or Rome it meant a sort of ambulant baby sitter, a slave who took children to school, taught them outward manners, saw to it that they did not fall into sin and difficulties, as, for example, homosexual relations, and otherwise looked after them before leaving them at the door where their true education took place. In the Greek comedies and on Roman reliefs, the *paidagōgos* is always described as a harsh, uneducated slave, who, for example, holds a little school boy a couple of inches above ground by his ear. Thus "custodian" is a more adequate and accurate translation than "tutor." The law in this argument served as such a custodian until the coming of Christ. And why? Because—or since Paul always saw things from the point of view of how God drives his history forward, *hina*, "in order that,"—"the law was our custodian until Christ came, (in order) that we might be justified by faith" (3:24). To be justified by faith is a possibility only in Christ. "But now that faith (Christ) has come, we are no longer under a custodian; for in Christ Jesus you are all children of God, through faith. For as many of you as were baptized into Christ, have put on Christ" (3: 25–27). Note the shift from "we" (Paul and his fellow Jews) to "you" (the Galatians).

Paul by this reasoning concludes that all are one in Christ and that there can be no divisions between Jew or Greek, slave or free, male or female; all are heirs to the promise to Abraham (3:28–29). This is pretty plain language, and it expresses quite precisely what I intend by my almost flippant image about the refrigerator. The strange thing is, however, that in the whole history of the Western tradition, particularly since Augustine, this passage has been read to mean absolutely the opposite of what Paul said. What do we mean in our dogmatic traditions when we say that the law is "our tutor unto Christ"? We mean that every Christian, to become a Christian, has to be tutored by the law in order to recognize his shortcomings, his guilt, so that he might thus really recognize that he needs a Christ, a Savior, a Messiah. But this is really to turn the whole thing upside down. When Paul says that the law has come to an end, he is arguing for the possibility of coming straight to Christ, not through the tunnel and funnel of the law.

How then did we arrive at our introspective, clever Western interpretation? Because we thought that when one reads the word of God, one should perceive the message as coming directly to us, and when the Bible says "we" and "our", we had better take it personally. The law, it says, was or is "our tutor" or "our custodian." Who am I then to say, "The Scripture says 'our,', but in this case it refers to a time back there, and not to me." But "our" in this text means, "me, Paul, with my Jewish compatriots," and nothing else. It is totally wrong to apply that "our" to *us Gentiles*. Of course, when we read in Acts "And then we sailed to Crete," very few preachers suggest that "we" should be understood as dealing with persons now, but as soon as such a pronoun occurs in a theological context, we fall into the pattern of applying it to ourselves. Many of Paul's uses of "we" and "our" are that stylistic plural by which he really means only himself, but in many cases, much more serious and difficult to detect, the uses of "we"—"we Jews"—stand in direct contrast to "you Gentiles." Romans 3:9 is a case in point: here the RSV translates the Greek "we" by "we Jews." It is important to develop a sensitivity to these distinctions. If one reads Paul as the called—not the converted—Apostle among Jews and Gentiles, not simply concentrating on him as the greatest theologian of the New Testament and the Protestant hero of deep theological thought, one might even be able to read the Bible and come to a more accurate understanding of what he wrote in his own time and to his own situations. That is the first condition for subsequent applications to our own times and situations.

3 Justification Rather Than Forgiveness

If one looks into a Greek concordance to the New Testament one is struck by the fact that in the Pauline epistles "justification" (*dikaiosunē*)—and the words related to it e.g., "to be pronounced and treated as righteous," "be acquitted" (*dikaiousthai*), and "righteous," or just (*dikaios*)—are pervasive in certain strata of Paul's thought. But the word "forgiveness" (*aphesis*) and the verb "to forgive" (*aphienai*) are spectacularly absent from those works of Paul which are authentic and genuinely of his own writing. A form of "to forgive" occurs only once within the main epistles of Paul (Rom. 4:7) and in that case poor Paul could not avoid using a verbal form, "were forgiven," because he had to quote Psalm 32:1 in which it occurs. He hastens on in this passage, however, avoiding the reference to forgiveness and using instead his favorite term "righteousness" or "justice" (Rom. 4:9). The term "forgiveness" does occur once each in Colossians and Ephesians, letters which stem from a writer much in the Pauline tradition but most probably not themselves authentic letters of Paul. In any case, in both Colossians 1:14 and Ephesians 1:7, "forgiveness" stands in apposition to and as an expansion or explanation of the term "redemption."

In spite of all this, however, forgiveness is the term most used both in the pulpit and, more generally, in contemporary Western Christianity to describe the sum total, the fruit, and the effect of the deeds of Jesus Christ. When we preach or when congregations talk together, it is forgiveness through Christ to which we bear witness. There are few in these times who would say to each other, "Have you experienced the propitiation of Christ?" Justification, redemption, salvation, reconciliation, propitiation—these are words which are somehow too theologically loaded, even though some insist on them as a badge of orthodoxy. When it really comes down to it, quite frankly, it all amounts to forgiveness. That is the way we feel about it, and why should we be bashful about our feelings?

One sometimes wonders, however, why there is such a strong emphasis on forgiveness, and I guess one of the reasons is that we are endowed with a strong psychological tendency in our minds and interests. We do possess a strong psychological bent, and there is no question that *the* term in any quest for relief from sin and guilt which works best within a psychological framework is "forgiveness." What makes this sort of quest so central—and again I guess—is that it is related to the fact that we happen to be more interested in ourselves than in God or in the fate of his creation. This is a general description —not necessarily a condemnation—of what Christianity is about today. We are so sure, and find it obvious, that God can take care of his own business, that our attention is quickly turned to anthropology. This concern appears easier, more natural, and in a line with much of Christian experience. Rudolf Bultmann's whole theological enterprise has *one* great mistake from which all others emanate: he takes for granted that basically the center of gravity—the center from which all interpretation springs—is anthropology, the doctrine of man. This might in fact be so, but if it be so it certainly devastates and destroys the perspective of Pauline thinking.

Once we confess our basic anthropo-centricity and psychologizing tendencies, then we have a key to the apparent lack of emphasis on forgiveness and the apparent emphasis on justification in Pauline thought. One might be dissatisfied with this since the term "to forgive" is found frequently in the rest of the Bible. It must be Paul who somehow has a blind spot here—if it be a blind spot. "Forgiveness" and "to forgive" occur in the Gospels and in Acts, they occur in Hebrews, James, 1 John, and in Revelation. Forgiveness is indeed a biblical term, inherited from the Old Testament and frequent in the Jesus tradition. It occurs, furthermore, many times in passages which certainly are not psychologically, anthropologically tainted. It is, however, this psychological, anthropological tendency which I must fight all the time as I try to understand Paul. I must work at the much harder task of trying to be fair to Paul, forgetting all I know of a long Christian history and experience in order to paint Paul's thought in true first century colors. Why is it that Paul speaks of justification and what does he mean by that term?

We must turn again to the concordance. It will be immediately observed that "justification," and words related to it by its root, are spectacularly predominant in one of Paul's epistles, Romans, in which they occur about fifty times. There are fewer but highly significant references in Galatians (thirteen times), and a few occurrences in 1 and 2 Corinthians and Philippians (about fifteen in all). The peculiarly Pauline connotation of the term "justification," *justification by faith rather than works*, is confined to Romans and Galatians, particulary to Romans. One might explain this by saying that it was only when Paul wrote to the Romans, perhaps his last epistle, that this peculiar significance came through to him. But for other reasons I do not think this is the case. There are hints of the term's significance in his earlier writings, and these are not tentative insights which only later seem to materialize, but rather indications, albeit not elaborated, which already show maturity of thought. My simple answer to this problem is that Paul's doctrine of justification by faith has its theological context in his reflection on the relation between Jews and Gentiles, and not within the problem of how *man* is to be saved, or how man's deeds are to be accounted, or how the free will of individuals is to be asserted or checked.

Among passages about justification by faith, two are most commonly cited: Romans 3:28 and 1:17. The RSV translation of Romans 3:28 reads: ". . . a man is justified by faith apart from works of law." (Luther's translation added "man is justified by faith *alone*." He wanted to make it truly Lutheran! Perhaps, though, he was right—in a way. He was at least no wilder in his translation than the New English Bible in which we find "a man is justified by faith quite apart from success in keeping the law.") In the course of Paul's argument in Romans 1:17 he cites Habakkuk 2:4 and the RSV renders the citation, ". . . as it is written, 'He who through faith is righteous shall live' or, 'the righteous shall live by faith.'" I would rather exploit the future tense of the verb "to live." Thus I would paraphrase the Greek: *There will come a time when the righteous will live by faith.*

Those two passages from Romans are the two classical ones, but there are many others. Noteworthy is the fact that wherever such passages concerning justification by faith occur in Paul's letters they most probably are to be found in the same verse as or at least adjacent to a specific reference to Jews and Gentiles. Thus Romans 3:28–29: "For we hold that a man is justified by faith apart from works of law. Or is God the God of the Jews only? Is he not the God of Gentiles also? Yes, of Gentiles also?" Similarly, Romans 1:16–17: "For I am not ashamed of the gospel: it is the power of God for salvation to every one who has faith, to the Jew first and also to the Greek. For in it the righteousness of God is revealed through faith for faith; as it is written, 'The righteous will live by faith.'"

Such examples alone do not of course, prove our point. Perhaps it would be more instructive to note how Paul discusses the Adam/Christ or first Adam/last Adam (Christ) typology or parallelism, once in Romans (5:14) and once in 1 Corinthians (15:45ff.; cf. 15:22). In Romans 5 the doctrine about Adam and Christ is woven into an interesting argument about justification. In 1 Corinthians 15 there is not a hint of justification in relation to the Adamic doctrine. This indicates to me that the doctrine of justification is not *the* pervasive, organizing doctrinal principle or insight of Paul, but rather that it has a very specific function in his thought. I would guess that the doctrine of justification originates in Paul's theological mind from his grappling with the problem of how to defend the place of the Gentiles in the Kingdom—the task with which he was charged in his call.

It is significant that it is in the Epistle to the Romans where much of this material on justification by faith is found. What is the Epistle to the Romans about? It is about God's plan for the world and about how Paul's mission to the Gentiles fits into that plan. The central chapters of Romans are neither the third nor the seventh, the latter being the one we read most anthropologically—where we Christians outdo the psychologists. "I do not understand my own actions. For I do not do what I want, but I do the very thing I hate. . . For I know that nothing good dwells within me, that is, in my flesh. I can will what is right, but I cannot do it. For I do not do the good I want, but the evil I do not want is what I do . . . Wretched man that I am! Who will deliver me from this body of death?" That is how *we* quote Romans 7:15, 18f., 24. But that is not what Paul says. He says, "I do not understand my own actions. For I do not do what I want, but I do the very thing I hate. Now if I do what I do not want, *I agree that the law is good*. So then *it is no longer I that do it*, but sin which dwells within me . . . So I find it to be a law that when I want to do right, evil lies close at hand. For *I delight in the law of God* in my inmost self . . . (Rom. 7:15, 21f.). Thus Paul does not feel responsible for sin; he is on the side of God! He does not get a "Protestant/Puritanical kick" out of this passage at all. Nor does he give it an autobiographical or existential touch. He simply uses an argument known from Stoicism and other ancient philosophies to show that the ego is on God's side, and that it recognizes the law as good. This point is clearly not the epistle's center of gravity.

The real center of gravity in Romans is found in chapters 9–11, in the section about the relation between Jews and Gentiles, the mystery of which had been revealed to Paul (Rom. 11:25 and Gal. 1:12; cf. Rom. 16:25). There is finally only one thing which was revealed to Paul as a mystery, as a specific revelation received neither from man nor from man's teaching but through Jesus Christ (Gal. 1:12): to preach Christ among the Gentiles (Gal. 1:16) with apostolic authority. That this is the mystery made known to Paul by revelation is well summarized in Ephesians where the deutero-Paulinist asserts that "the Gentiles are fellow heirs [with the Jews], members of the same body, and partakers of the promise in Christ Jesus through the gospel" (Eph. 3:6).

In Romans 9–11 Paul frequently cites Old Testament passages which bring to mind the hope that if all Israel believed in the promised Messiah and embraced him, then everyone—including the Gentiles—would be saved. But the glorious secret that was whispered into the ear of Paul the Apostle, the Jewish apostle to the Gentiles, was that God in his grace had changed his plans. Now it was the "No" of the Jews, their non-acceptance of the Messiah, which opened up the possibility of the "*Yes*" of the Gentiles. Particularly in Romans 11 does Paul point out that ultimately when the full number of Gentiles have become God's people, then by jealousy (Rom. 11:11) the Jews will also be saved (11:15, 25–27). The central issue claiming Paul's attention is that of the inclusion both of Gentiles and Jews.

It is useful in this context to consider the account in Acts of Paul's behavior in his missionary ministry. Whenever Paul went to a new city, Acts depicts him as going first to the synagogue where he preaches, albeit with little success. Only

a few women follow his message (Acts 16:1, 14; 18:2), and
to a Jew of the first century that represented no great success.
Paul's message was generally rejected by the Jews (Acts 13:
43–45, 14:1 f., 17:1–7), and consequently from the synagogue
he went out to the market places in order to preach to the
Gentiles. This appears to be a pattern. Now a professor of
missions might tell us that this demonstrated that Paul was a
great strategist: he used the synagogue, to which he had access,
as a starting point from which he could then broaden his activities. But I rather think that Acts intentionally records this
pattern: Paul had to register the "No" of the Jews before he
was allowed to bring the gospel to the Gentiles. This is what
is theologically expounded in Romans 9–11.

To the central revelation of these chapters is then appended,
so to say, a preface—Romans 1—8, in which Paul argues that
since justification is by faith it is equally possible for both
Jews and Gentiles to come to Christ. In that preface he does
not deal with the question of how man is to be saved—be it by
works or law or by something else. He is simply pointing out
in a very intelligent and powerful theological fashion that the
basis for a church of Jews and Gentiles has already been set
forth in Scripture where the prime example is Abraham:
"Abraham believed God, and it was reckoned to him as righteousness" (Gen. 15:6 as cited in Rom 4:3). In Romans 1—8
both Gentiles and Jews are found equally culpable (Rom.
3:9ff.), yet also equally capable of being saved through justification (Rom. 3:21–30).

The course of this reasoning may be clarified by examining
the messianic expectations in Paul's days. In the Jewish
discussion there were two possibilities for the time of the
coming of the Messiah: *either* the Messiah would come in an
age of perfect righteousness when all of God's people obeyed
the law, *or* the Messiah would come in a time of extreme iniquity. In eschatological and apocalyptic literature there is
nothing grey—there is only white or black, salvation or condemnation, heaven or hell. And so also in the expectations of
the Jews: the Messiah would come in a time when people are

either totally pious or completely guilty. Paul, having recognized that the Messiah had come, needed neither the insights of sociology or psychology to know that the time was not completely good—hence it was utterly bad. That is what he argues in Romans 1. The Messiah had come and the time was not one of goodness but sinfulness. Not only has a righteousness of God been revealed (Rom. 3:21), but the wrath of God has also appeared (Rom. 1:18). This wrath of God is, so to say, the other side of righteousness, of justification. Paul describes in rather grim colors the depravity of the Gentile world, a description built not on sociological studies but on the very obvious theological premise that things had to be utterly bad. And then he proceeds to show that the Jews with the law are in no position of advantage and have no reason to brag (Rom. 2), since the whole world is under the power of sin (Rom. 3:1–20). This being so, Paul concludes, it is about time for the righteousness of God to be revealed. "But *now* the righteousness of God has been manifested apart from law . . . the righteousness of God through faith in Jesus Christ for all who believe. For there is no distinction; since all have sinned and fall short of the glory of God, they are justified by his grace as a gift . . ." (Rom. 3:21–24).

Why does Paul use the term righteousness/justification? The same Greek word is involved (*dikaiosunē*)—but the term seems peculiar, unnatural and difficult to understand. We are quite accustomed to hearing the phrase "justification/righteousness by faith," yet that very phrase sounds strange unless we understand the background of justification/righteousness. The background is Hebrew. The Hebrew word is found in what Old Testament scholars consider to be the most ancient part of the Bible—not in Genesis 1 but in Judges 5, the Victory Song of Deborah. A literal translation of Judges 5:11 reads, "There [by the watering troughs] shall they rehearse the (*tsidhqoth*) righteousness of Yahweh . . ." The KJV reads "righteous acts"; the RSV, "triumphs"; the NEB, "victories" or "triumphs"; the JB, "blessings"; and the NAB "just deeds" of the Lord. Of course, they are all correct—in a way—but some tend more toward a literal meaning of the word and others perhaps toward a more correct or easily understandable interpretation. How can it be said that the people rehearse the righteous acts of the Lord? What are the the righteous acts of the Lord? It is the fact that God vindicated his people against their enemies. And why is this called a righteous act? Can a bloody, dirty war be a righteous act? This *is* evidently the sort of thing that is being celebrated.

The fact is that Judges 5:11 refers to a situation, a time, or a mood in which a group of people, a nation, or tribe is absolutely convinced of its identity as God's people. Any manifestation of God's righteousness must therefore mean that this people is exalted and triumphant and that its enemies are defeated. If this people is God's people, then, when righteousness comes, it must mean salvation, triumph, victory, blessing, and the destruction of the enemy. This is plain and simple, because God's righteous act means that God is putting things right—and that is *tsedaqah*, the righteousness of God.

When we follow this term through the Old Testament, we see how it takes on another meaning in some of the prophetic writings. Thus, for example, when Amos is not so sure that that the so-called people of the Lord are true Israelites, truly keeping their covenant responsibilities, God's righteousness cannot or does not mean vindication, but rather condemnation. Hence the line of demarcation between right and wrong, faithful and sinner, makes the Day of the Lord not always a glorious, triumphant white day of light for God's people when God's righteousness manifests itself. The day of the Lord is darkness and not light (Amos 5:18) and he predicts judgment, a punishment for an iniquitous people who have broken God's covenant.

This "day of the Lord," the day of eschatological judgment, develops in an interesting way in the history of the Christian Church—especially in those happy churches which have indulged in the beautiful playfulness of varying the colors for altar, pulpit, lectern hangings, and vestments in order to char-

acterize the changing seasons of the liturgical year. Christmas
and Easter, for example, are seasons of joy and triumph and
white is used. Advent and Lent, times of preparation and
repentance, use violet. Festivals reminiscent of the Holy Spirit
such as Pentecost and martyrs' days use red. Green, the color
of nature and nurture, is used for ordinary seasons such as the
long series of Sundays after Pentecost which serve to teach
Christians about their ordinary ethical obligations. Black may
be used for deep mourning as on the occasion of a funeral, or
for Good Friday. Now the church year starts with the first
Sunday in Advent and is preceded by the Last Sunday after
Pentecost (sometimes called the Sunday before Advent). This
last Sunday of the church year is usually given over to medi-
tation on the day of judgment, "the day of the Lord." In the
history of the church that day has had all the colors of the
liturgical spectrum—white, as a triumphal joyful day of vindication; black, as a mournful day of fear and condemnation;
violet, as a day for repentance and penance; and green, mark-
ing an ordinary day when people continue to live a Christian
life with the idea of final judgment remaining quite remote.
It all depends on how the church sees itself. Is the church
really the elect people of God? If so, then of course the coming of judgment is, as for the early church, a joyful event to be
anticipated and a day of victory yearned for, a day of vindication, a white day of triumph and light. And this describes
perhaps not only the very early church but also those churches
which today consider themselves to be a small faithful minority
of God's elect. When judgment is spoken of, it is a glorious
day.

In contrast, the more established the church has become, the
more uncertain its holy arrogance reveals its claims to heaven
to be. Then the day of judgment becomes dark and threatening—perhaps black, certainly purple! A prophetic corrective
to too much certainty and a sign of the need for repentance
take precedence over any joyful assurance that God's coming
in final judgment will be vindication. Such a prophetic corrective runs through the Bible and now seems particularly

appropriate in our time of injustice and in our situation when we often need to be prodded by a prophetic voice out of complacency. Anger is often associated with the prophetic message, with the righteous wrath of a prophet who speaks for the Lord against those who have broken covenant.

In the Rabbinic tradition this penetrated even more deeply. The righteousness of God is not described there as redeeming some and condemning others, but rather as the line of demarcation which goes through the heart of every person. There are two impulses fighting within man: the good impulse, *yetser tob* and the evil impulse, *yetser ha-ra'*. Such a concept, of two warring impulses or inclinations within the individual, represents quite a sophisticated development. It is a rather handsome awareness to see that it is somewhat superficial to consider that everyone will be saved, or that some are to be saved and others not. The line thus must pierce through each individual's heart. This is a mature doctrine. But the originators of Christian faith did not benefit from such a higher education in theology. What is seen in primitive Christianity is again, as in the Essene sect at Qumran, a clear awareness that those who are loyal to the community and to its leader are precisely those who will be saved. At Qumran, loyalty to the sect of the new covenant and to the Righteous Teacher were determinative.

In a similar—sectarian—way the early church set loyalty to Jesus Christ and his messianic community as the key to salvation. There may be danger of apostasy—but each and every little irregularity of the individual Christian did not really threaten the hope of salvation. To be cast out of the church, really excommunicated, happened but rarely and the offense had to be extremely grave. There is only one case of expulsion from the church in Paul's epistles—and even that case is not one of definite and ultimate excommunication. In 1 Corinthians 5 an instance of incest is recorded, and Paul says, "Let him who has done this be removed from among you" (1 Cor. 5:2), yet he is convinced that if the offender is delivered to Satan for the destruction of the flesh in order to save his

spirit, his spirit is yet to be saved on the day of the Lord
(5.5).* In any case, this incest case is the only one of straight
excommunication.

Thus in the early community there was a certain amount of
elasticity; those who were members would remain so and
could expect salvation. Therefore when one spoke of the manifestation of God's righteousness, God's *tsedaqah*, it was a
word of salvation. As in the Song of Deborah in earliest
times, it meant, salvation, rescue, victory, triumph. Here we
have the chief reason for Paul's emphasis on the terms, justification and righteousness. This emphasis presupposes a faith
in which the church knows itself as belonging to God, knows
its enemies to be God's enemies. There is a certain arrogance
to this but it is at the heart of covenant faith. And in such
a setting, that term righteousness/justification (*tsedaqah,
dikaiosunē*) once again took on its whole glorious meaning.
One of the most ancient liturgical prayers preserved from the
early church is found in a small early second century writing,
the *Didache*. There, in a Eucharistic prayer of thanksgiving,
we read: "Let your grace come and let this world pass away
. . . *Marana tha*, Amen." Freely translated this means: Let
this dirty world go to pieces and let your kingdom come . . .
O Lord, come! The consummation with its judgment was
anticipated in joy. Hence God's righteousness was not a
judging but rather a vindicating righteousness, i.e. you were
justified, you were vindicated, and you shall be saved.

As we have noted in respect to Paul's use of call rather
than conversion, and justification rather than forgiveness, his

---

* Proper translation of those last words is of general importance for Bible translation. The RSV and most translations use a subjunctive expression here: "that
his spirit *may be saved*. . . ." Such "may be" language suggests a degree of
uncertainty in the mind of the contemporary reader. But the Greek subjunctive
"may be saved" (*sōthē*) is simply governed by the rules of Greek grammar
which state that the conjunction "in order that" (*hina*) is to be followed by
the subjunctive mood. Such a subjunctive suggests no uncertainty but rather
the divine purposefulness: in order to have the spirit saved! The subjunctive
mood of English Bible translations is pervasive in such cases and has led to
the destruction of the tone of happy assurance of biblical faith. Whenever,
therefore, we read "may" and "might" we should make sure that we are not
deprived of that assurance by literalistic translation.

language is quite different from our contemporary speech. But it is precisely *his* language and original meanings which in these chapters we are attempting to recapture and revitalize. The problem I am addressing—and I may not be completely right, but I do have a chance of being correct at some vital points—is what did *Paul* actually mean? What did *Paul* actually think? It is not so much the question of what the words in themselves might mean, but rather the more important distinction, which tends to be confusing if it is not made clear, between what the terms meant in their original usage and how they might be used now. Thus, we must go back to the period in which the Pauline material was written and study the backgrounds of these terms in the Pauline context and time. This is important for anyone who works in the biblical field. When it is not done we frequently miss noting clearly enough the differences between what Paul consciously intended and what his words have come to mean in our usage.

Many of us read the Bible all on one level. One reason for this may be that we are somewhat afraid that unless we do this the word of God is not going to be relevant for us. We do not have enough faith in the word of God really to allow it to speak for itself—so we hang on our own little relevancies, just as apples or other decorations are hung on a Christmas tree. Actually, there is no greater threat to serious biblical studies than a forced demand for "relevance." We must have patience and faith enough to listen to and seek out the original's meaning. If this is not done, biblical study suffers and may, indeed, come up with false and faulty conclusions and interpretations.

In my own Swedish tradition there have been many wonderfully "relevant" sermons through the ages. I am reminded of one delivered in the eighteenth century, when pastors were asked by the government to foster the introduction of the potato to Swedish farmers, and consequently sermons were often preached on the text, "Man shall not live by bread alone." Another emphasis was on the hygienic aspects of life and a sermon was once preached on the pericope of the widow's son in Nain (Lk. 7:11–17) with the title "On the Advantages of Placing Cemeteries outside the City." Now these were very "relevant" sermons and the points they made were valid in the community of faith, for God does care for nutrition and health. Of course, they seem funny to us—yet a far funnier fact is that one rarely laughs when "more spiritual" relevancies than these are tagged on to the interpretation of texts. As soon as it "sounds pious," anything can be tagged on. The relation between the Scriptures in their original meaning and their meaning for us here and now is, indeed, *the* problem on which countless serious biblical scholars and systematic theologians are now focusing. Often there is a sort of slogan or password by which one is proven to be really in the club, in the swing of things: it used to be *eschatology*, and then for a while it was *kerygma*, now it is *hermeneutics*, i.e. the methods of interpretation.

This is a serious point for our topic because we have gone behind the hermeneutical to the exegetical level—behind today, behind Luther and Calvin, behind Augustine. We have tried to see an original meaning—albeit an original meaning which proved by interpretation and reinterpretation to be significant at different points in history. But when is it legitimate to read Paul's words about justification or about, say, conscience in a truly Pauline mood, a mood which seeks to discover what was in the mind of the *author* rather than meanings for us today? As an exegete, a biblical scholar, I must be primarily concerned with the former question. But as a theologian and pastor let me point out that we are not supposed continually to play "Bibleland" and dream ourselves back into a sort of Semitic mood. That is not what God wants us to do. But, we must *first* read the Bible to find original meanings and allow those meanings to correct our tendencies to read our own views into the original rather than letting the original stand and speak for itself. Seek ye first the original meanings—and all these things shall be yours as well . . .

It is very important, for example, that when Paul speaks about the Jews, he really speaks about Jews, and not simply the fantasy Jews who stand as a symbol or as the prime example of a timeless legalism. Already in the Gospels we can detect a tendency toward symbolic "type casting" of the Jews, especially in John, or in Matthew's term "the scribes and the Pharisees," or in Luke's image of the Pharisees as the prime example of wrong piety. But in Paul's letters the real Jewish people, his own people, are in focus when he shapes his argument about justification by faith.

When I preach to people in the New England area, where there is a substantial Jewish community, and I say to my Christian hosts that Paul would at best call them honorary Jews—for that is what a Gentile Christian is, according to Paul (Rom. 11:17ff.)—this does not meet with universal approval, to say the least. When I tell Gentile Christians who live in a good and affluent suburb that only by adoption are they honorary Jews, they are startled. And when I claim that Romans 9—11 deals with our relations and attitudes to the Jewish businessman who has moved in next door, they simply find me odd and unspiritual. Such Christians have gone to the proper church schools and learned all the things that Paul says concerning the Jews. But what they have learned does not concern Jews in the flesh. Indeed, they still identify the Jews with the stereotype. And here is a case where, perhaps, it might be that what Paul actually spoke about in his letters, particularly Romans, is indeed to be applied to the relationship between Jews and Christians in this age and in this country. The United States of today is the first place in the modern world since Philo's Alexandria where Jews and Christians as people, as religious communities, and as learned communities, live together in a manner and in sufficient numbers to allow for open dialogue. It is the first time in recent history where there could be an open relation between Christians and Jews and where the conversation which Paul started in Romans 9—11, but which was broken off mainly by Christian expansion and superiority feelings, can start again. The pain of history and the shame of the holocaust interfere with real dialogue, but the possibility really exists and, it is to be hoped, will increase.

If we carefully observe Paul's writings, it might even be

noted that the Bible speaks about real Jews, and not only about
an emasculated prototype of legalism. There is another aspect
of this: if what Paul says about Jews and Gentiles becomes
absorbed into a typological description of the salvation of individual souls, we find things to be something like this: (1)
obedience to the law, (2) the manifestation of Christ, and
then (3) a development to higher things beyond the law. It
is as though everyone for a while is a Jew, a legalist, and then
after the coming of Christ one is saved. Somehow, seen in
this way, something has been lost of the feeling of the once-for-
all nature of the history of salvation. I once heard the preacher
in my home parish, a Lutheran Church where the Rev. Henry
Horn is pastor, preach on the famous text about the laborers
in the vineyard (Mt. 20:1–16). All the laborers—even those
who had come in only at the eleventh hour—receive the same
payment for their work. This seems hard and unjust. So the
preacher, Dr. Horn, first gave the usual boy scout message:
the Boy Scout does his duty without consideration of reward,
and this is usually augmented by the Protestant slant, i.e.,
Jesus in that parable intimates that one should not really think
about different rates of rewards because the one and only true
reward is Jesus Christ, salvation itself. But Pastor Horn is a
good preacher who reads his Bible, and I paraphrase what he
finally said: "But of course that is actually *not* what the text
is about. Do you know who the eleventh hour folks are?
They are we, the Gentiles. It was Israel who worked through
the whole long heat of sacred history and we lazy Gentiles
came in at the last moment and got the same pay." That is not
so different from Paul's perspective in Romans 9—11.

Finally, on a more traditionally theological level, what about
the need for a sense of failure under law and sin as the way—
the only way, as it is sometimes suggested—to experience the
reality of salvation through Christ. What are we to make of
it when it is suggested that the chief role of the law is to
accuse us—*lex semper accusat* as they said in the 16th century? Did Paul think the only way to become a good Christian was out of frustration and guilt?

It seems to me that Paul was a pretty good Christian. He may not really have been attractive; he was not a sympathetic sort of fellow; he was certainly arrogant. But he was great! And Paul did not go through the valley of sin and guilt; he went from glory to glory. It may be that the axis of sin and guilt is not the only axis on which Christianity revolves. (See following, Section 4: "Weakness rather than Sin".) When I read the New Testament, I have the feeling that what we now deal with in church is too often a little private matter of individual ethics, and that is really small business when compared with the greater issues people really have on their minds. I certainly do not like the sin of adultery. It is no good, but it is hardly the main problem of the world. Yet people so often feel the church considers adultery to be *the* problem. There are many horror movies making the rounds these days with enormous popularity—"Jaws," "The Godfather," "The Exorcist, "The Towering Inferno"—and I have wondered why. There are Freudian and other psychoanalytic explanations. But in my judgment, I think we are all frightened of our confused world—sensing deeply the unrest among nations, possible national catastrophe, the threat of nuclear, natural, or economic disaster. And it is reassuring to be able to withstand terror on the movie screen for a couple of hours— very reassuring.

Now it so happens that the New Testament also has a script for a horror movie, the Book of Revelation. That in itself is something of a key to the fact that our age and that age of the first century have more in common than we think. We share not only a search for individual peace and inner harmony and salvation, but also a wider and more pervasive generalized anxiety. Both times can be characterized as cosmically scared, frightened ages, caught under principalities and powers where tiny little human beings just know that they cannot do much, that they are not in control, that they are just caught. That is one of the aspects of Christianity which might be opened up with the help of Paul—if we restore Paul to his fullness and do not translate him into a biblical proof-text for Reformation

doctrines. Thus even justification by faith, important though
we have seen it to be, must be subsumed in the wider context
of Paul's mission to the Gentiles, part of God's total plan for
his creation. Or perhaps we should say it this way: Paul's
thoughts about justification were triggered by the issues of
divisions and identities in a pluralistic and torn world, not
primarily by the inner tensions of individual souls and consciences. His searching eyes focused on the unity and the God-
willed diversity of humankind, yes, of the whole creation.

4 Weakness Rather Than Sin

There are very good reasons to see Paul as an Apostle, not
simply as a super-Christian; and as a man with a robust conscience, not plagued by much introspection. Such an image of
Paul could easily give the impression of a hard-hitting, efficient
agent to whom personal experience added little or nothing to
his understanding of the faith, the Lord, the Church—or himself. It could also lead to an image of Paul as a triumphalist,
a person whose already abundant earlier achievements are
crowned with the new glories and possibilities given by Christ.

But both of these images would be far from the truth.
Paul's personal experiences are constantly woven into his
understanding of the mission and the faith. Triumphalism,
moreover, is the mark of his *opponents*, not of himself. The
point where Paul's experience intersects with his apostolic
mission and his understanding of the faith, furthermore, is not
"sin" with its correlate "forgiveness." It is rather when Paul
speaks about his weakness (*astheneia*) that we feel his deeply
personal pain. Once more we find something surprisingly
different from the Christian language that most of us take
for granted: it seems that Paul never felt guilt in the face of
this weakness—pain, yes, but not guilt.

It is not in the drama of the saving of Paul the sinner, but
it is in the drama of Paul's coming to grips with what he calls
his "weakness" that we find the most experiential level of

Paul's theology. More importantly when Paul speaks about weakness, he does not think of sin (with one possible exception, mentioned below, pp. 47–48). I stress this promptly and strongly so that we keep weakness and sin apart. Otherwise the impression might be that I am referring to sin when actually I am referring to weakness—quite a different matter. In our time we tend to equate the two. When Paul speaks about being strong when he is weak (2 Cor. 12:10), and about the ways in which he recognizes his weakness, we tend to read this "weakness" language as a sign of his deep insight into the sinful predicament of humanity. That would be a modern misunderstanding.

The classic passage about Paul's weakness is in 2 Corinthians 12, where Paul contrasts his glorious spiritual experiences with that weakness of his which he describes as "a thorn given me in the flesh, a messenger of Satan, to harass me, to keep me from being too elated" over the abundance of revelations he had received (2 Cor. 12:7).

Since Paul is an original and not merely an apologetic theologian, he speaks with some uncertainty about which heaven it was he visited, and he also speaks with some proper theological hesitation about whether this experience was in the body or out of the body (2 Cor. 12:1–6). Such modesty—or intentionally ironic narration of a marvelous experience designed to put that experience in proper perspective—has often been forgotten in some theological circles that pride themselves on being biblical. In such circles it seems that admission of uncertainty endangers the authority of faith. Here is another issue of "weakness" which Paul's opponents feared—while Paul came to see it as the proper stance, lest the power of God be confused with the assured style of the speaker—and thereby obscured.

Having spoken about this experience, which was no doubt glorious and genuine, Paul says that there remained a thorn in his flesh, an angel of Satan to buffet him, which taught him the lesson that God's grace was sufficient for him and that somehow God's strength was more evident through his weakness than through his strength. Three times Paul beseeched the Lord to be relieved from this thorn (2 Cor. 12:8–10). I always find that interesting. Why only three times? That does not seem to represent much if this problem was a serious concern to Paul. Three is a sort of semi-holy number frequently used in biblical thought, and that may be sufficient reason for his choice. I tend to think so. The number might also represent the few occasions when Paul had gone out into the desert to make a real retreat, a Promethean battle of prayer with the Almighty, prayer fasts about this thorn in his flesh.

I am given to believe that it is most reasonable to consider this thorn in the flesh as an actual sickness. My argument does not depend on that, but I think it is the most reasonable interpretation. And personally I am not against the suggestion—which is not awfully well grounded—that this might have been a condition of epilepsy. It might, to be sure, have been something else, but that Paul's sickness was somehow a serious handicap to his ministry seems rather clear. It was so for many reasons. It is always hard to be sick, especially while traveling. But for a great man, charged with such a momentous task as Paul thought himself to have, it must have been especially difficult to accept that God would allow such a handicap when he knew that Paul was such an important person. It should have been God's business, to keep at least this apostle in fit shape so that with his great ability he could do as much as possible in the ministry for the Lord. But there is more to it than that: the view of the early church was that sickness is really a sign of a lack of that renewing power of life which is the very essence of the Christian existence. A sick apostle is almost like a one-legged football player, a contradiction in terms, because sickness was really a sign of the powers of the old age at work to doublecross the work of God.

We know how seriously sickness and its next step, death, was looked upon by Paul when he says to the Corinthian church that since they have practiced segregation at their communion, "some are sick and some have even died" (1 Cor.

11:30). And we know how the Thessalonians were quite shaken in their faith when some Christians started to die. The way in which Paul had preached the gospel certainly had given them the impression that everyone would remain healthy up to the day of the Parousia, the Coming of the Lord in glory. And the Thessalonian correspondence was directed precisely to correct such an overinterpretation, so to say, of the powers of life available in the gospel (1 Thess. 4:13ff.). There is no question that Paul himself expected to be around at the Parousia; though doubtlessly sick, he would nevertheless be around. 1 Corinthians 15:52 clearly says that those who have died will be raised and *we* shall be transformed, which certainly presupposes that Paul is on that *we* side which will not have tasted death before the coming of the Parousia.

The clearest reference to illness as a handicap in Paul's ministry is, however, Galatians 4:13ff. where he praises the Galatians for not having taken offense at the fact that he was stranded in Galatia because of a bodily ailment. But in spite of his illness, in spite of his sick condition, they accepted his message as the word of God. It is clear from that passage that sickness for an apostle represents two or three strikes against his being a full-fledged, sound, genuine bearer of that power of life which is the gospel. And this might also be involved in 1 Corinthians 2:3, where he speaks about how he brought his gospel in weakness; it might refer too, I think, to what he mentions in 1 Thessalonians 2:18, ". . . we wanted to come to you—I, Paul, again and again—but Satan hindered us." I think he was just plain sick, and could not go. It was that angel of Satan, the one who was smiting him in the face, whom he refers to in 2 Corinthians 12.

The weakness of which Paul speaks is one that comes to him—into him—from without. It is Satan's attack, the dirty double-crosser who tries to impede God's work. We could call it a martyrological weakness, i.e. the weakness of the martyr, not due to his or her shortcomings but to outside opposition to the martyr's witness. All of this must have been very hard for Paul. It was a real thorn in the flesh, this weakness, but he sees it not in relation to his personal salvation but precisely in relation to his ministry, its style and its effectiveness.

At no point in his main correspondence do we find an intimation that Paul had any kind of bad conscience in relation to this weakness. He never said, "I am weak, I am wretched; humanity is weak; weak and sinful is my existence." There is no identification of the weakness or illness of the apostle with sin, and Paul has no inclination to search his innermost conscience about some secret sin which might be the cause of this weakness or sickness. On the contrary, he finds his weakness one of those things which makes him one with the Lord, and which makes his ministry a true ministry of Jesus Christ who was crucified in weakness. Precisely in his weakness is he one with the Lord who died in weakness, he who "was crucified in weakness" (2 Cor. 13:4). In this weakness the power of Christ's resurrection spreads through the missionary message to the church and manifests itself. Paul's sickness is a little—and perhaps not so little—Golgotha, a Calvary of his own.

This line of thought is intensified in one of the writings close to and growing out of Paul's thought, the Epistle to the Colossians. It is expressed there in terms which are difficult and even shocking to theologians: "Now I rejoice in my sufferings for your sake, and in my flesh I complete what is lacking in Christ's afflictions for the sake of his body, that is, the church" (Col. 1:24). To any proper theologian this must be strange language. Of course, neither Paul—nor indeed anyone else—could add anything to the work fulfilled once for all on Calvary. Yet in Colossians 1:24, Paul's ministry in its weakness, its martyrological suffering, is seen as having the same nature as the afflictions of Christ, afflictions that "continue" in the church and are thereby completed (cf. also 2 Cor. 13:3-4).

Further, in 2 Corinthians 4, we encounter a problem in reading the Pauline letters which was referred to earlier on page 23, namely the problem of distinguishing what "we" means in various passages. This question must be faced if Paul is to be read as he intended. If 2 Corinthians 4 is examined carefully, it provides a classic example of how this "we" language must be understood. This is a long passage in which Paul uses first person plurals quite clearly to mean "I, myself, Paul," i.e. simply first person singular. "For what we preach is not ourselves, but Jesus Christ as Lord, with ourselves as your servants for Jesus' sake" (2 Cor. 4:5)—the "we" (Paul) and "*your* servants" (the congregation addressed) in this verse are quite clear. And it is actually Paul, speaking about his own revelation in Jesus Christ, who continues, "For it is the God who said, 'Let light shine out of darkness,' who has shone in *our* hearts to give the light of the knowledge of the glory of God in the face of Christ" (2 Cor. 4:6).

Clarification of whom the "we" refers to is important, because it is necessary to be very careful lest we regard revelations to great apostles as exemplary for rank and file Christians. In the New Testament there is a difference in Christ's church between the apostle and the ordinary foot-soldier. This distinction is of particular importance in traditions which have retained the heritage of Pietism and revivalism. The expression, for example, "to meet Jesus" only makes sense when there are actual experiences of such a meeting involved. But as poetic language which describes going to church, it is dangerous language. It is far too strong and perhaps almost dishonest to describe our worship experiences in such inflated terms. There is much in our religious jargon which always makes me think that we often fall for the temptation which David, the young shepherd, withstood when he refused the offer of Saul's great armor before he met Goliath in battle. There is much rattling of oversized and cumbersome Saul-like armor on our little David-like souls and minds. And we would be much better off if we had the same simplicity in our preaching, speaking, and prayer as the young David had when he smote that Philistine with a single stone from his slingshot. So, we should be careful with this "we" and "I." We should not extend or extenuate such language for the description of general religious experience. Paul has something very specific and unique in mind: His own peculiar call and mission.

Paul continues (2 Cor. 4:7–9): "But we [i.e. I, Paul] have

this treasure in earthen vessels . . . We are afflicted in every way . . . persecuted . . . struck down. . . ." And all these uses of "we" are primarily relevant only to Paul. We should be very cautious when we democratically transfer them, democratizing them and using them for our average situation. In 2 Corinthians 4:10 Paul says that we (i.e. Paul) are always "carrying in the body the death of Jesus." It is not so much the marks of death which Paul bears as the process of dying—and this makes him one with the suffering Christ. Now I do not say that this cannot apply to us—by humble analogy—but if we really want to feel the specificity and the reality of this language, we should initially confine it to Paul. Here is the sick and weak Paul, pitted against the healthy, sun—tanned apostles whom he fights in Corinth. It is Paul who refers to himself—not to every Christian, but to himself—as "carrying the death of Jesus in my body, so that the life of Jesus may be manifested in our bodies" (2 Cor. 4:10). He continues, "For while we live we are always being given up to death for Jesus' sake, so that the life of Jesus may be manifested in your mortal bodies. So death is at work in us, but life in you" (2 Cor. 4: 11–12). Paul, thus, is on the weak and dying side, while the congregation is to be endowed with life and renewed. While Paul, so to say, is the "cross," the congregation is the "resurrection." There is much more power and specificity in this when one reads it as really related to Paul and his weakness.

It is almost exclusively in the Corinthian situation that Paul deals with this concept of weakness, just as it was almost exclusively in Romans—and to some extent in Galatians—that Paul speaks of justification. Thus we again note how this great theologian has a large variety of ideas which he applies when needed. Paul has but one overriding idea and one monotonous pattern which he follows regardless of the situation addressed. Paul places this view of weakness in which God's power manifests itself, over against the "super-apostles," the *hyperlian apostoloi* (2 Cor. 11:5, 12:11), with whom he is in such serious controversy. This is found particularly in the last part of 2 Corinthians (as we read it in our Bibles), chapters 10–13.

The polemic of 2 Corinthians 10–13 against agitators in his Corinthian community—his so-called "letter of tears" (cf. 2 Cor. 2:4, 7:8)—is intended both to return the church to unity and to defend his own authority. It is strong polemic in which Paul, probably writing from Macedonia stressed and guarded his apostolic authority. He was at a distance and able to write with strength, stressing his own adequacy and ability. But when this rather small, ugly, sick man actually appeared on the scene he seemed not to carry much weight. The super-apostles are reported to have said, "His letters are weighty and strong, but his bodily presence is weak, and his speech of no account." (2 Cor. 10:9). Paul, who described himself as tired, afflicted, fearful and downcast (2 Cor. 7:5–6), has to plead with a congregation which has fallen into the hands of slick operators, the seemingly successful missionaries who had come to Corinth and were challenging both Paul's authority and his basic teachings. It is in this context that he speaks about his weakness.

In 1 Corinthians weakness is placed over against knowledge (1 Cor. 1:5) and wisdom (1 Cor. 1:17, 19 *et passim*), interestingly it is in 1 Corinthians 1 (note especially vv. 17–18) and only there that Paul uses the famous words that Christ sent him to preach the gospel "not with eloquent wisdom, lest the cross of Christ be emptied of its power" (1 Cor. 1:17), and ". . . we preach Christ crucified. . ." (1 Cor. 1:23). Paul wants nothing but Christ crucified—no frills, no extras, no frosting—Christ crucified, "the weakness gospel." Luther stressed the *theologia crucis* (theology of the cross) over against the *theologia gloriae* (theology of glory). Lutherans wisely maintain his suspicion of all triumphalism—be it in Corinth or in Rome or in Washington. The theology of the cross, the theology of weakness, is really part and parcel of Paul's deepest religious experience in a ministry related to his own weakness.

There is, however, one passage, and as far as I know only one passage, where weakness stands parallel to sin, namely, Romans 5:6ff. There a trilogy appears: "While we were yet helpless [lit.: weak, *astheneis*], at the right time Christ died for the ungodly . . . God shows his love for us in that while we were yet sinners Christ died for us. Since, therefore, we are now justified by his blood, much more shall we be saved by him from the wrath of God. For if while we were enemies we were reconciled to God by the death of his Son, much more, now that we are reconciled, shall we be saved by his life" (Rom. 5:6–10). We can paraphrase and summarize this: "While we were yet *weak*, Christ took the initiative and died for us; while we were yet *sinners,* Christ took the first step; while we were yet *enemies*, Christ took the initiative so that through his death we were reconciled." Paul goes on to say that if we are now justified, then certainly God will be able to take it from there. The big step was to get this weak, sinful, enemy into the *status justificationis*, into the status of justification, where there is salvation. Christ did this by lifting Paul into the new eon. The point is that when Paul here speaks of weakness, he speaks of it as something past. Now it might be possible that, in this passage in Romans, Paul consciously uses this word in a sense different than when he speaks about his weakness in Corinthians. It should always be remembered that the different letters of Paul address differing situations, and his language and message are thus couched in varied terms, or, perhaps, in the same terms with varied meanings. This is not because his letters are separated from each other by a few years, but rather because they are real, pastoral letters directed to specific situations. Thus, in the Corinthian correspondence when Paul speaks about his weakness, it is in the context of some specific argument about his own authority, aimed against his opponents, and designed to stress the theology of the cross. He sees his weakness, his sickness, and the difficulties or shortcomings of his ministry as related to his weakness and as that which teaches him about the nature of Christ's ministry in this world and the nature of Christ's power in this life. When writing to the Romans, to a congregation he did not as yet know and one which he had not founded, Paul uses weakness in a more general way, and as part of his argument for justification.

One should also note that there is in the New Testament what might also be described as a weakness motif, a motif perhaps to be described as the "nonheroic" note in Christianity. One quickly recalls heroic Christianity in relation to temptations, trials and tests, as often noted, "Count it all joy, my brethren, when you meet various trials, for you know that the testing of your faith produces steadfastness" (James 1:2–3). Such a passage can, for example, be used to show that temptation is equipment in the gymnasium of life to strengthen the muscles of faith. But such a heroic Christianity, is far from the center and actually alien to the spirit of Christ.

Jesus did *not* teach us to pray "Strengthen us in the moment of temptation," but "See to it that we do not fall into temptation." In the Lord's Prayer, we read, "And lead us not into temptation, but deliver us from evil (or: the Evil One)" (Mt. 6:13 cf. Lk. 11:4b). Were we to hold that an Aramaic original stands behind the Greek of this prayer as transmitted in the New Testament, the verb "to lead" might possibly have a form in Hebrew and Aramic which could be rendered "Do not *cause us to be led* into temptation." The more recent translations of the Lord's Prayer are right in preferring the word "test" rather than "temptation"—the Greek *peirasmon* has both meanings. A paraphrase would then be: "Do not let such a situation come to pass in which we find ourselves put to the ultimate test," is more in keeping with the Gospels, since a Christian is there portrayed as knowing that when Satan, the Evil One, pulls out all the stops there is no chance that a person can stand (Mk. 13:20, par. Mt. 24:22). In the Gospels there is nothing heroic about fighting Satan as far as the followers of Jesus are concerned. The Gospels are too realistic about Satan's powers. The only help is divine intervention—that for the sake of the elect the time of ultimate testing be shortened since no human being could otherwise be saved (Mk. 13:20 and par.). This is the mood of the Gospels, in which one does not take an heroic attitude toward persecution, toward temptation, toward the attacks of the enemy. It is significant in this regard to consider Matthew 10, a chapter which brings together a missionary charge to the disciples and instructions about their mission. The tone of the charge is nonheroic: "If anyone will not receive you or listen to your words, shake off the dust from your feet as you leave that house or town," "When they persecute you in one town, flee to the next . . ." (Mt. 10:14; 10:23a). The disciples are not told to put up a fight. This is clearly nonheroic. Of course, if the situation is desperate and the disciple is delivered up and dragged before hostile authorities, he has no choice—and even then it is not his valor but the Spirit of the Father speaking through him that will bear testimony (Mt. 10:19–20).

To the Corinthians Paul sounds the same note: "God is faithful and he will not let you be tempted beyond your strength, but with the temptation will also provide *the way of escape*, so that you can endure it" (1 Cor. 10:13). And when Paul lists his own hardships—beatings, being stoned, shipwrecked, in all sorts of dangers, discomforts, and anxieties—even as he boasts, he refers to his own weaknesses (2 Cor. 11:23–29). But when he comes to the end and draws his conclusions, he has saved a little nugget of his experience which he places as a sort of final image before his congregation: "If I must boast, I will boast of the things that show my weakness . . . At Damascus, the governor under King Aretas guarded the city of Damascus in order to seize me, but I was let down in a basket through a window in a wall, and escaped his hands" (2 Cor. 11:30–33). I do not think that I overexegete when I say that Paul consciously saves that experience in order to portray the way he wanted the church to know him: unprepossessing, ugly Paul, on the retreat, sneaking out, crumpled in a basket. That is the image of the apostle of Christ. That is the earthen vessel, which does not allow the glory of God to be overshadowed by cleverness, by achievement, by healthiness, by any martyrological urge to make a stand: ". . . we have this treasure in earthen vessels, to show that the transcendent power belongs to God and not to us" (2 Cor. 4:7).

Thus, Paul perceives his weakness not as something that comes from within himself—lack of obedience, sanctity, or moral force and achievement. Rather, his weakness comes from without—it is inflicted by Satan, it is an infliction of the enemy. Once again we see Paul's robust conscience. Yet it is more than that; it is a way of perceiving and a way of living which, in a most powerful manner, became the very matrix of both his Christology and its application to his ministry.

One might speculate on where all this leaves us. Some things are obvious. Negative observations are, perhaps, the most interesting. Paul's is a totally different domain of discourse, a totally different way of looking at weakness, than the introspective, self-centered, anthropological vision to which we have become accustomed. It is also clear that there is built into his way of thinking a deep suspicion against all that is spectacular or successful—against all that stresses prestige in the ministry.

Having said that, and now finding ourselves two thousand years later, we must be careful lest we be led astray. We recall that Jesus told a story about a tax-collector and a Pharisee and it was the tax-collector who was justified because of his humility (Lk. 18:9–14). Once we mention that Jesus said, "every one who exalts himself will be humbled, but he who humbles himself will be exalted," then there are difficulties in getting people to sit up front in church—because, of course, they desire to appear humble. We have been told that we should be like the publican rather than the Pharisee—but the more we try, the more pharisaic we become. A vicious circle is set up which is hard to break.

We have a similar problem with weakness, especially whenever we think we have occasion to boast in our weakness. There are many temptations for ministry at this point Some of us have a tendency, when we do not do our work and things crumble and do not go well, to say, "Now that is because I am not as superficial as the minister in the church next door who is so popular and who draws such a large congregation. People do not want to come and hear me, because I am preaching the *real* gospel, and I am being a *true* minister. Did not Paul himself have similar experiences in Corinth?" It takes much wisdom and clarity not to fall into the pitfall of hearing a great apostle's insight into his weakness and then turning this

insight upside-down by cheap imitation. This we cannot do—
be we pastors, teachers, or anyone trying to fulfill a vocation.
Martin Luther was right when he discussed this problem of
weakness and the cross: "All right! A Christian bears his
cross, but he is not the one who picks it. He is not the one
who decides what sort of cross he is going to bear." Anyone
who lives his or her life in ministry will, no doubt, have real
reasons for knowing weakness—his or her own thorn in the
flesh, which often, however, is not the one it appears to be.
To bear one's cross is to accept it in meekness without frustration. Luther usually described this—and perhaps he overdid
it—by saying that it is much easier for a monk to go through
his ascetic, world-denying observances at set times and in an
orderly way, than it is for a minister to have all kinds of inter-
ference from the spouse or the children precisely at that
moment when he feels he should be doing something else.
Although this is a small example, it is not totally irrelevant.

Let me now return to the larger issue. I have tried to
picture what Paul might have meant when he spoke about
weakness rather than sin. This is the most *experiential* factor
in all Pauline theology. Without a consideration of this
theme it might appear as though I am against experience *qua*
experience—which is not the case. Paul is, to be sure, the
truly perceptive intellectual among the apostles and the New
Testament writers. He really had a passion for clear theoretical
thought concerning justification and other theological issues.
Yet there is also a very personal, human Paul—the Paul we
have considered in this chapter. That Paul speaks to us of
weakness rather than sin.

5 Love Rather Than Integrity

The title, "Love Rather Than Integrity" is, perhaps, more difficult than those of the preceding chapters in that it contains the
word *love*. "Love" is a particularly formidable term in that
it often is used to sum up the whole gospel, the whole mean-

ing of the life, suffering, and death of Christ, the whole content
of the Christian message. It is often taken for granted that
love can express almost everything of importance in many
areas. Few words suffer more inflation, not only in our language but also in our thoughts and feelings. Much of the
Christian message was caricatured in the Charlie Chaplin movie,
"Limelight," in which the lyrics of one whole song consisted
solely of a constant repetition of the word "love," this heavily
charged word, "Love, love love . . ." Or, perhaps closer to
home, the song, "For They Know We are Christian By Our
Love," is so catchy and delightful—for a while. It is interesting to reflect on the reason why one tires of such a song
rather quickly; and it might have something to do with the
inflated use of the word "love."

Yet I must warn myself and others against being put off by
what we regard as cheap and diluted. To many it seems as if
deep and true theology consists in ridiculing the Golden Rule
as a center of the Christian faith. It is as though a split ought
to be created between the "deep theologians" and the more
popular proponents of Christianity. This often leads to sneer-
ing at a summary of the Christian life as expressed in the
Golden Rule, and overstresses the importance of the theology
and theory of God's love as exemplified in Christ's life, suffering, and death. It may also be possible that the Golden Rule,
"So whatever you wish that men would do to you, do so to
them; for this is the law and the prophets" (Mt. 7:12, cf. Lk.
6:31), is seen by the deep theologians as acts rather than love,
as legalism, or as really no more than a utilitarian bargaining
which demeans the pure command of love. So we do have a
delicate matter here. How does one speak about love? How
can we avoid theological elitism on the one hand, and inflation
or vulgarization on the other?

The classical text where Paul speaks about love is, of course,
1 Corinthians 13—the hymn of love, to love, for love. The
King James Version's rendition, "charity" may have served
its purpose in the 17th century, but in the 20th century it has
taken on a meaning other than that which was originally

implied. To distinguish between "charity" as *works* of charity, actions of love, in contrast to a mere *attitude* of the heart or feeling is good, and well in keeping with Paul's intention. "Charity," however, has come to mean condescending alms-giving, the self-serving gift of the rich to the poor—and that dimension is certainly not what Paul had in mind. It rather seems as if that was what he was criticizing, "If I give away all I have, and if I deliver my body to be burned, but have not love [KJV: charity], I gain nothing" (1 Cor. 13:3).

What is Paul speaking about? If we use the methodology and presuppositions of the preceding chapters, we should try to determine not what *we* might feel but rather what Paul seems to be saying as he explodes into semi-hymnic language at this particular point in his argument with the Corinthians. We are told that without love no deeds—not even the greatest deed of giving oneself to be burned as a martyr or as a sacrifice on the altar—would count for anything, would be of any ulti-mate use.

One level on which 1 Corinthians 13 can be read, and I think it is the level on which we usually and naturally read it, is this: Here is the great insight that deeds, even the great-est of deeds, can grow out of inferior motives, can be means of self-assertion even to the point where we may morbidly wallow in false images of our own Christian virtues. Then it is that only the inner and ultimate motivation—love—really counts. Modern theologians would then be happy to point out that the Greek word in 1 Corinthians is *agapē*, the unmotivated love of God, so totally different from what the world usually calls "love," i.e. *eros*, the aspiring self-seeking love of human beings. One of my compatriots, Anders Nygren, has written a very perceptive study, *Agape and Eros,* which points out and uses this important distinction. Accord-ing to his ethical and motivational interpretation of 1 Corin-thians 13, Paul asserts that any works or deeds, any spectacular manifestations of spiritual power in prophecy or speaking in tongues, are of no avail unless they flow out of that non-self-serving, real, unmotivated fountain of love.

From this base, one can easily arrive at deeper psychological insights which recognize that all the really important things, all the "virtues" which really count are but by-products of *agapē*, that love which cannot be commanded volitionally or created out of pure cognition. One cannot love by willpower alone. No one can tell himself, "Now I will love," and then proceed truly to love. Love is beyond our control.

It is, perhaps, easy to see the difficulties inherent in such a mechanism as it relates to humility, one of the trickiest, funniest virtues of the Christian life. There is a well-known story about a man who wanted to be humble: "He was very happy when he managed to be humble. But he was very *sorry* that he was happy that he was humble. And he was very *happy* that he was so sorry that he was happy that he was humble . . ." And there is no way whatever out of that vicious circle, since humility once possessed is lost, since humility is precisely that which grows out of knowing one's poverty. There is something of this visciousness connected with love, something of it connected with everything in the world which really counts in relations between people. Love is simply *there* under certain circumstances. I guess some philosophers or theologians would say that love is a relationship rather than a *habitus* which can be held in one's hand. Love is, perhaps, more of a radiation, a wave phenomenon, rather than matter.

We are very sensitive in these matters, and anyone who has any religious insight knows how useful such perceptive analysis is. The point is that love given without love is an insult, condescension, mere charity which is humiliating. I am reminded of St. Vincent de Paul, the Roman Catholic counterpart of General William Booth, the founder of the Salvation Army. St. Vincent started a sort of slum mission in France in the 17th century, devoted to the care of prisoners, the sick, the abjectly poor. I still remember a wonderful movie about him many years ago, *Monsieur Vincent,* and it may have appeared here under some other name. At the point in the film where Vincent dies, after having started organizations to help in the worst slums in Paris, he says to the Sister who watches with him at his death bed, "Sister, we must love these people very much, so that they can forgive us for having helped them." There is much wisdom in that. Love as an action, even when it means that I offer everything that I possess and give it to the poor—but without love—would be nothing in our great Western tradition except a burden and an insult.

This concern for help which is non-humiliating is an insight with far-reaching significance in the political realm, in terms both of domestic and of foreign policy. It explains why the "charity" model of helping the needy does not work. It does not work for the simple reason that it is not "love" as long as the ego (collective or individual, we/I) wants to remain in command, to call the shots, to be in control. True love demands that neither the giver nor the receiver be conscious of giving or receiving. One could say that payment of taxes as a means of alleviating the discrepancy between the rich and the poor is imaginative obedience to Jesus' words concerning the giving of alms: ". . . do not let your left hand know what your right hand is doing . . ." (Mt. 6:3). For in paying taxes we give, but we are deprived of the satisfaction of saying, "I give." That is closer to love.

We could interpret Paul along these lines for quite some time and we would find much in 1 Corinthians 13 which seems to point in that direction: If I did all good things, but not out of genuine love, it would avail nothing. Then, however, we would start to wonder why the chapter has so much about understanding mysteries, about knowledge (*gnōsis*), about prophecy, and speaking in tongues (1 Cor. 13:2,8). Such notions do not fit naturally into the message of love, according to the interpretation we have chosen to pursue thus far. Yet they do force us into the context of the epistle as a whole, and especially into the chapters immediately preceding and following 13. We should, of course, have started our interpretation with the whole epistle in mind—but I wanted to show that I could play the Western game of introspection, too, and thereby reveal the way in which it would point.

The general context of the epistle is the problem which

Paul had in Corinth about the excitement, the enthusiastic extremism, and the magnificent achievements which some Corinthians seemed to experience. The church of Corinth was actually a glorious church, but it was far from an ideal church. There were few churches, it seems, with which Paul had such terrible problems—but perhaps that is just an accident of the correspondence and its collection.

Corinth was a seaport, a city, a metropolitan area not dissimilar to other cities of the Hellenistic world into which Christianity made its way. The image of Corinth as a sinful city is often epitomized in commentaries and sermons by reference to the fact that the Greek verb, *korinthiazesthai*, "to live as in Corinth," came to mean "to practice fornication" because Corinth was famous for its courtesans. That is correct, and Aristophanes may have coined that phrase as part of the Athenian disdain for the south during the Peloponnesian War. There is, however, no indication that Paul's Corinth was especially wicked. His city was totally new, founded as a Roman colony in 44 B.C.; the old Corinth had been destroyed a century earlier. It was in this great and confused city that Paul preached his gospel, and there it took hold. And while there were many problems, it was never dull. The Corinthians really excelled—in all kinds of things: in speaking in tongues, in prophecy, in shouting, and in all manner of sins as well. Paul's First Epistle to the Corinthians addresses itself to this problem. The chapter immediately preceding the one on love deals with the Spirit, the one Spirit which has many gifts (1 Corinthians 12). In this chapter Paul strangely affirms that speaking in tongues is no more a gift of the Spirit than is teaching or even administration. That there is nothing more spiritual in speaking in tongues or prophesying than in sitting behind a good and responsible administrator's desk is an interesting statement. Perhaps they had no desks then, but they certainly had the same contempt for administration as every preacher or teacher or student has in our time. Paul seems to be trying somehow to show that all these go together. Thus when he refers to *agapē*, love, he is actually saying that any spiritual achievement, any Christian deed, any Christian virtue apart from *agapē* can be detrimental, dangerous and threatening to the well-being of the church. There is a wonderful passage in Colossians which gives a summary of this thought: "Put on then, as God's chosen ones, holy and beloved, compassion, kindness, lowliness, meekness, and patience, forbearing one another . . . and forgiving each other . . ." (Col. 3:12–13). And after listing all these solid and glorious virtues, the writer makes the main point: "And above all these put on love, which binds everything together in perfect harmony" (Col. 3:14). If one pressed the imagery, one might say that if the bond or belt of this love does not engirdle the Christian, these fine virtues might be a cause of stumbling or tripping. And anyone who knows how difficult it is to live with virtuous people understands the point.

Love, then, is not the "super-virtue." Love, to Paul, is constant concern for the church, for one's brothers and sisters. This is the point: concern for the church, for one's fellow Christians is what love is about. Knowledge (*gnōsis*) makes one boast or have pride, (1 Cor. 8:1), while love builds up (*oikodomein*, to strengthen, edify [the church]). This strengthening, edifying love is what 1 Corinthians 13 deals with. Love, not in the sense of *feeling* ever more deeply into one's innermost emotional life, but love in the sense of plain, reasonable concern for the church in its totality is the greatest of things. Even speaking in tongues or giving so small an amount as the widow's mite is a threat to the strengthening and structure of the church unless done within the totality of the *oikodomē*, the building up of the Christian community, God's edifice. Thus Paul finally says, "So faith, hope, love abide, these three; but the greatest of these is love" (1 Cor. 13:13). Of course, one could skeptically suspect that what is happening to Paul is what happens to every preacher who tells his congregation every Sunday morning that the topic he is now going to speak on is the very center of the Christian message— there are many such "centers." But I do not think that we are dealing with that kind of rhetoric here. Paul means exactly what he says. He does not place attitudes or virtues or gifts of God side by side—we must have faith, we must have hope, we must have love. He rather points out precisely that it is love which keeps even things like faith and hope from deteriorating into little lapel buttons which we flaunt to proclaim our own cleverness, our own commitment, or our own capacity to believe and trust. In reality, love means actually to be what one is together with one's brothers and sisters to the benefit of the building up of the church.

I have entitled this chapter "Love Rather Than Integrity," not because I have anything against integrity, and not because the Bible considers integrity a sin. Integrity is the issue when people with different views and different convictions and different gifts must live together. This can become a problem, and Paul addresses precisely this problem when he emphasizes love. What are the specific issues in 1 Corinthians? There are many. It is a particularly interesting epistle because Paul had so many specific matters to take up. He often begins a section by saying, "For it has been reported to me that . . ." (1 Cor. 1:11); "It is actually reported that . . ." (5:1); "Now concerning the matters about which you wrote . . ." (7:1); "Now concerning the unmarried, I have no command of the Lord, but I give my opinion . . ." (7:25); "Now concerning food offered to idols . . ." (8:1); ". . . I hear that there are divisions among you . . ." (11:18); "Now concerning spiritual gifts, brethren, I do not want you to be uninformed" (12:1); "Now concerning the contribution . . ." (16:1); In effect, he writes, "Now as to the matters you wrote me about concerning so and so, these are my views." He takes up matters of divisions, incest, marriage, the unmarried, food offered to idols, segregation at the Lord's Supper, spiritual gifts and the collection for the Jerusalem church. Such questions—regarding church discipline, marriage, what sort of food to eat, different spiritual gifts, etc.—are all prompted by the situation in the church in Corinth. Paul writes concerning what he has heard and he deals with the questions which have been addressed to him for clarification.

The issue concerning which Paul most clearly demonstrates the relation between love and integrity is the one about food. Once more I stress that although this problem is one we do not have to face in our time, we must understand what the question meant to the Corinthians in Paul's time. The situation was that much of the meat available in the meat markets of Corinth came from the temples. Very little of the meat from the animals of sacrifice was actually consumed in the temples, either by fire or in sacred meals. The vast majority of all such meat was sold on the open market in Corinth. The question which plagued the church was whether this meat, having been sacrificed to idols, is something a Christian can eat without being tainted by idolatry. That is Paul's problem in 1 Corinthians 8—10.

It is interesting to note that Paul does not deal with any of these questions by saying, "Have you not learned that I am against legalism? Therefore there is no problem. It is solved." For some reason Paul does not make use of that "most Pauline" insight. Rather, he states a principle with a far more pragmatic slant (1 Cor. 6:12): Everything is allowed me, but not everything is helpful for the community, i.e., for the building up of the church. This principle is also stated in 1 Corinthians 10:23, and there it is even more clear that he has in mind the building up of the church: everything is allowed, but not everything builds up. Both times the principle is applied to controversies about food—not the Jewish-Christian controversy of kosher food (Acts 15:20, cf. Gal. 2), rather the question of eating of "food offered to idols."

On this matter different Christians in Corinth had different views. Some, "the strong," claimed the freedom to eat such food—and Paul considered them theologically correct. But others, "the weak," held such practice to be wrong. In these passages Paul urges the strong not to flaunt their freedom, but to be governed by the concerns of the weak. Actually the whole of 1 Corinthians 8—10 is governed by the principle: I have great rights, but I have learned not to use them to the hilt. Paul's reflection on the strong and the weak is repeated in a more stylized form in Romans 14, a chapter which begins by urging the strong to accept the weak—but not for the purpose of disputing with, despising, or judging and debasing them. There Paul stresses even more strongly the importance of respect for one another's convictions. The church is a place where people can afford to live together with different views, but that requires love. It is in a climate of love and mutual acceptance that respect for diversity is heightened to the final statement: anything that does not come out of conviction is sin (Rom. 14:23, cf. 14:5).

Of course, the Christian is free to eat food which had been offered to idols, because he knows the idols to be nothing. Of course, Paul or other traveling apostles could receive a salary for their work, because the Old Testament states that when the ox treads out the grain it shall not be muzzled (Deut. 25:4), and Jesus, when he sent the disciples out on their missionary task said that the laborer deserves his wages (Lk. 10:7, 1 Cor. 9:14). But Paul preferred not to make this claim and thus maintained an occupation with which he supported himself when he went about his journeys. He reasoned that a Christian has many privileges but he is under no obligation to take advantage of them, particularly if such advantages cause trouble to others—especially to the weaker members of the church. Thus, Paul does not make maximum use of his privileges, of his freedom, because it might cause factions in Christ's church. No Christian can insist on integrity, even of conscience, if it works to the detriment of those for whom Christ died (1 Cor. 8:9–11).

The gist of Paul's thought is that integrity is of no value in itself, integrity should not be put on display. The Christian should refrain from many privileges for conscience's sake—not for the strong Christian's conscience but for the conscience of that other Christian who may be weak and for whom a privilege may become a stumbling block. To order one's life by the conscience of the other weaker person, is the extreme example of love rather than integrity. This is all to be seen in the overarching perspective of the building up of the church. Thus

Paul is led to say something which we may not find attractive:
To the Jews I became as a Jew, in order to win Jews . . . To
the Gentiles I became as one outside the law, so that I might
win the Gentiles . . . To the weak I became weak, that I
might gain the weak. I have become all things to all men . . .
(1 Cor. 9:19–22). Were this made into a general principle,
it would be abhorrent and certainly lacking integrity. Even
though it is for the Lord and for the mission it seems wrong;
itself lacking integrity, such a statement produces problems.
Perhaps there is a good way and a bad way to accomplish
what is good . . . but is this only an ego trip for Paul? What
is important, however, is love—concern for the community—
rather than integrity. And this really presents difficulties and
dangers. Are we afraid of disturbing the peace? Are we
afraid of being powerful and forceful witnesses?

The history of Christianity provides an ample quantity of
answers to these questions as it is observed in relation to religious, theological and social issues. I lecture about the Bible
to many ministers who say, "Oh, it's wonderful for us to dis-
cuss these fine points here, but of course I couldn't really speak
in this way to my congregation. It's not because of my conscience but because of theirs." This is a real problem and we
must face it and be frank about it. There are times when I
am not so sure as to who are the weak and who are the strong.
It is not so certain that those who hold back should always be
identified as weak. It may sometimes be the other way around.
In any case, though, I must describe Paul's principle: love
rather than integrity.

The ultimate importance of love is also evident in the Gospels. In Matthew 25:31–46 there is the grandiose image of
the last judgment, the separation of the sheep from the goats
when the Son of man comes in his glory—the sheep at his right
hand and the goats at the left. Jesus there provides an interesting criterion for those who will be judged to be at the right
hand: "Come, O blessed of my Father, inherit the kingdom . . .
for I was hungry and you gave me food, I was thirsty and you
gave me drink, I was a stranger and you welcomed me, I was

naked and you clothed me, I was sick and you visited me, I was in prison and you came to me . . . Truly, I say to you, as your did it to one of the least of these my brethren, you did it to me" (Mt. 25:34–40). The usual way, I guess, of preaching on this text is to say that Jesus here pictures what will happen at the final judgment so that people can behave accordingly. At this level, however, an interesting theological problem arises as to how such a criterion accords with the doctrine of salvation by grace, since here salvation seems to depend on works. Perhaps we could hold, as some do, that this refers to judgment within the church alone, and not all humanity. And as we read on to the end of chapter 25, we might get a psychological kick out of the fact that those who did the right things did so without knowing it, and those who did the wrong things also did so without knowing it; those who were remiss did not see Christ, those who showed concern also did not see Christ. This can be cleverly exploited—"This is the way it is with really good deeds. They are done unknowingly—from *quellende Liebe*, love that simply wells up and overflows— much as that unmotivated love, *agapē*." Such an interpretation of Matthew 25:31–46 may be correct, but I doubt it. I think, rather, that these words about the last judgment are thought of by Matthew as a farewell speech of Jesus. Our Lord is not saying, "You, my followers, are interested and concerned with the last judgment, so I shall give you instructions as to how you will be saved." Rather, he is saying, "Friends, I am going away; and now I shall show you that I make the little ones, your brothers and sisters in the church, my representatives, my stand-ins. It may be that you would like to serve me out of gratitude, but I tell you to put that service to the community and particularly to those who are the least in it." That is why the dialogue: "When did we see you hungry and thirsty and in prison and came or did not come to you? Truly, I say to you, as you did it/did not do it to one of the least of these my brethren, you did it to me." Such an interpretation dovetails with a principle of love in which the whole religious effort is directed to the community.

When I stress love rather than integrity I also stress a widened, broadened conscience so that we can see all our brothers and sisters, indeed all humanity as objects of our loving concern. This will bring us out of our smugness and away from the kind of pride which was rampant in Corinth. That is not to imply that we should be preoccupied with deeply introspective, narcissistic egos, but rather that we must look around and see what is to the benefit of the community. Our ethic must be aimed toward the totality of the church rather than toward a depraved and self-directed ego. The ego and the conscience claim too much of our attention; "other-directedness," self-denying love succeeds better at being the main element in Christian life.

Some examples from the Gospels make this clear as, for example, the story about the Great Commandment (Mk. 12:28–34 par., Mt. 22:34–40, and Lk. 10:25–28). A lawyer (in Mark, a scribe) tests Jesus by asking him which is the great commandment, that which must be done to inherit eternal life. In the Marcan and Matthean accounts Jesus answers, but in the Lucan parallel Jesus turns the question back to his questioner who then responds with the double commandment: to love the Lord with heart, soul and mind and one's neighbor as oneself. This story, in turn, brings to mind the account of the rich young man (Mk. 10:17–31 par., Mt. 19:16–30, and Lk. 18:18–30, in which the man is a ruler) who asks Jesus what he must do to have eternal life, a question which Jesus answers by referring to the Ten Commandments. The young man responds that he has observed these commandments from his youth. One might expect that Jesus would have pointed out that the young man probably was taking a superficial view of his obedience and that he might actually have offended at some point. But this Jesus does not do. Rather, he demands one more thing of the young man which, although sorrowful about it, he cannot give—his many possessions hold him back from following Jesus. And in the Lucan account of the double commandment, after the lawyer has responded, Jesus says, "You have answered right; do this, and you will live" (Lk. 10:28).

In both narratives it would appear that the *doing*, works righteousness, is being stressed. Yet in both cases it is actually the attitude toward the neighbor, toward the poor or the outsider which is the central point. This is clear when it is seen how that Lukan answer is followed by the parable of the Good Samaritan (Lk. 10:29–37). There the point is that it is the Samaritan, the outsider, who proves truly to be a neighbor. It is the Samaritan who is not anxious about keeping apart from one he is supposed to despise, who is not anxious about his integrity. The Samaritan acts out of love, not heeding special interest and thus being free to be a neighbor to anyone in need. This is the special twist, the point of the parable; this is love rather than integrity.

I have always liked the story of the boy scout who knew that it is good to help old ladies cross streets. He had, however, really started to understand the seriousness of Christianity, so that he had started to realize that he did such good deeds—leading old ladies across the street—just to show off. One day there was an old lady who needed help in crossing the street, but the scout withstood the terrible temptation to help her because he knew he would be doing so only to show off. So he kept his integrity, and the old lady was run over. Indeed, he had kept his integrity but he had lost the perspective of love. Perhaps it is more important to help than to be totally pure in one's integrity.

The famous words which appear in the context of a passage on the celebration of the Lord's Supper (1 Cor. 11:29), "For any one who eats and drinks *without discerning the body* eats and drinks judgment upon himself," are also to be understood in terms of love, true concern for the other. This text has held a place of tremendous importance in the history of the Eucharist, the Lord's Table. Exegetes in our time are more or less in agreement that the way to understand the text must be in the context of the whole passage. The problem, then, concerns the celebration of the evening meal in Corinth, a city which was marked by a very wide sociological spread in its constituency. Upper class people came to the supper with elaborate meals—at least fancy sandwiches—but the slaves could not sneak out until very late, and then they could not bring any food unless they had stolen it. So Paul says to the rich? "Do you not have houses to eat and drink in? Or do you despise the church of God and humiliate those who have nothing?" (1 Cor. 11:22). Now to that mundane issue he adds, "For I received from the Lord what I also delivered to you, that the Lord Jesus on the night when he was betrayed took bread, and when he had given thanks, he broke it, and said, 'This is my body which is for you . . .'" (1 Cor. 11:23–26). The bread and wine are described as given to the disciples, and the words of institution are placed after Paul's rebuke of those who did not heed the poor. Then Paul returns to this issue and the thrust of judgment is put in terms of *not discerning the body*, something which is terrible. The Christian who by such behavior does not recognize the community of the church is liable to condemnation, and this is so serious that some are weak and ill and some have even died (1 Cor. 11:30). This is a breaking of love, of *agapē*. It is interesting that those passages about eating the bread or drinking the cup of the Lord in an unworthy manner so as to profane the body and blood of the Lord (1 Cor. 11:27), and not discerning the body and thus bringing judgment upon oneself (1 Cor. 11:29), are passages which have been tragically divisive in the history of the Eucharist. Actually they push in precisely the opposite direction from divison. We might paraphrase: "How can you practice segregation at Communion? Do you not recognize that you cut the body of Christ in pieces if there is segregation of any kind or for any reason at the Eucharist?" Church or ethical problems are really group or community problems, because Christianity is not a principle to be followed with utter clarity or precision. Christianity is an experiment in living together—and with a certain flexible ability to take differences into account without being divided. It might have been Paul's pharisaic background which made him so sensitive to this issue. Perhaps he had had enough of shining integrity and perhaps that really had done something to him to give him a vision of a new way of living. In such a life ethical problems and the whole existential problem of man become a life together under the one Spirit which by love holds the manifold gifts together —so that even the greatest of gifts serves not as irritation but as blessing. "And above all these put on love, which binds together in perfect harmony" (Col. 3:14).

As we have wandered through various demonstrations of Paul's principle, *love rather than integrity*, we may now be ready to rephrase it, and sharpen it by saying: love allows for not insisting on one's own integrity at the expense of the unity of the community. Love, as Paul understands it, urges us to respect fully the integrity of those who think and feel otherwise. In Romans Paul expresses it well when he says, "Welcome and accept the one who is weak in faith—and not for the purpose of arguing . . . Let everyone be convinced in his own mind" (Rom. 14:1,5). Love allows for the full respect of the integrity of the other, and overcomes the divisiveness of my zeal for having it my way in the name of my own integrity.

6 Unique Rather Than Universal

The most striking evidence for diversity in early Christendom is clearly the Apostolic Council described in Acts 15. To come to terms with that key event, however, one must also deal with Paul's report of the outcome of that council in Galatians 2. If what happened in Jerusalem was roughly what is reported in Acts 15, then Paul's understanding in Galatians, with its accent on the collection, is certainly a highly opinionated interpretation of the agreement described in Acts (15:20).

There is, of course, extensive debate in the literature— ancient and modern—about the relation between Galatians 2 and Acts 15. I find it reasonable to think that the "event" is the same, and we must free ourselves from the impression that Acts had the "actual" description and that Paul has bent the record into something more acceptable to himself and his mission. Both Acts and Paul remember the event as a crucial one. Both Acts and Paul remember that the matter was resolved to the mutual satisfaction of the Council and Paul. Acts sees it from the perspective of those who required a continuity with the Torah; Paul—especially in Galatians which reflects increasing pressure from the Judaizers—stresses that a commandment of circumcision was not enforced (2:3) and that the emphasis fell upon the demonstration of unity, symbolized by the collection for the Jerusalem church, a matter to which he often refers in his epistles (Rom. 15:25, 1 Cor. 16:1, 2 Cor. 8—9).

This all goes to show the uniqueness of Paul and his mission, and how he zealously defends the special task and perspective that had been given to him. In Galatians he bases this unique mission on his call to be the apostle to the Gentiles, a call, a task, and a gospel which he was not free to relinquish and which had also been recognized by others, even those who differed with him (2:6ff). They had extended to him and his mission the "right hand of fellowship" (2:9).

A model from 1 Corinthians allows us some insight into how Paul found it possible to work in his unique fashion while being aware of other missions and theologies. In 1 Corinthians 3—4 he reminds the congregation—and himself—of how parties that exist need not lead to schism (cf. 1 Cor. 11:18) if they remember that in the church such diversity is not to be seen as a debate like that between schools of philosophy (cf. Rom. 14:1)—that would be a carnal and merely human perspective, a secularized view of Christianity (1 Cor. 3:1–3). For the church is a spiritual reality, a mystery held together by God who in due time will sort out what is lastingly true. There is no need for resolving theological conflict before that time (4:5). Even if the results of bad theology come to naught and its perpetrators suffer a loss of prestige on the last day, they will be as much saved as those who teach good theology (3:12–15), as Paul thinks he does (4:4: "I know of nothing wrong with my teaching").

All this goes to show how Paul himself is aware of his uniqueness but also how he sometimes reflects on that uniqueness as it fits into the totality of the church. Convinced of being right, he nevertheless sees that only God can sort it all out, as he will on the day of judgment and consummation.

The traditional view of Paul is heavily influenced by the fact that he had such great success—after his death—in getting his letters into our Bible. Almost one third of the New Testament ultimately came to be ascribed to him, and plenty remains so, even if only less than half of that was actually written or dictated by him. This tended to reinforce an understanding of him as *the* Apostle to the Gentiles. Nothing would have pleased him more, yet it would have surprised him since all indications are that in his own lifetime he had far from such pervasive influence.

To be sure, the way the Book of Acts is structured contributed to this monumental perception of Paul. Yet from that book it is clear both that Paul is far from being the only vehicle by which the gospel reaches the Gentiles, and that the distinct accents of his message suffered some loss in the process of being incorporated into the pattern and scheme of Acts.

Perhaps the best way of getting at the question that must be raised at this point is to pose it somewhat like this: "If there had been no Paul, would Christianity have made it in the Gentile world?" I think anyone who is brought up in Christian schools is inclined to say that had not Paul come along, Christianity would have dwindled into a little Jewish sect, or something like that. Paul himself is very much inclined to think thus, and many of our textbooks back him up gloriously. But what are the facts? The answer is that Christianity may have made it, and made it very well, and furthermore, in the time when it happened, Paul's activities were actually a tremendously complicating factor rather than an asset for a pragmatically sucessful missionary program.

Look at the record: according to Acts, Stephen delivers a speech with a theology which has nothing in it whatsoever not exactly in accord with what he did: he went straight to the Gentiles initiating a successful mission (Acts 6–7). Cornelius, a Gentile, is converted far before and with no relation to Pauline theology. The church in Antioch was full of Gentiles and thrived long before Paul was called. There are other people—such as Apollos—mentioned both in Acts and in Paul's letters who were Gentiles or who worked successfully among Gentiles. Furthermore, Paul touched only a few centers of the early Christian movement. It was actually his principle only to touch those which nobody else had visited. (Rom. 15:20). Rome was a blossoming congregation, mainly Gentile, without his doing. He did not go to places already evangelized as, for instance, Alexandria, about which we know nothing but that it was thriving, or the churches of the East and the Aramaic-speaking parts of the church. And from Paul's own letters, we know that Corinth saw an enthusiastic response to those missionaries who did not pay heed to Paul's thought. What Paul brands "judaizing"—circumcision and dietary laws for Gentiles—was not a barrier to Christianity but quite attractive to Gentiles, who were enamored of what was Oriental. The Hellenistic world was full of the inroads of both the ferocious and the beautiful in liturgical, cultic, and sacramental procedures imported, for example, from Egypt and Syria. Even ritual laws like those from the Old Testament were not a liability but an asset—as any reader of Galatians can see. In Paul's epistles there is evidence that communities were eager to take on as much as possible of Leviticus, rather than dismissing its laws as a burden.

All our writings in the New Testament are directed to congregations containing Gentiles, and I would even go so far as to say that there is not a single writing in the New Testament which is not directed to a congregation which is primarily Gentile, including the Gospel of Matthew and the Epistle to the Hebrews. Practically all of the New Testament, including the Gospels, comes from communities that consisted either exclusively or predominantly of Gentile Christians—and most of them developed from the Jewish roots of the Jesus movement in ways untouched by Paul's mission and specific understandings. The gospel message was well accepted; why, then, should Paul come and complicate matters?

Now Paul's position was certainly unique. Yet he had little following since, on the whole, his reasoning was not

felt to be of help. It is sometimes said that Paul had only
one consistent follower and that he misunderstood Paul—Marcion. That is not quite true; it is an overstatement. But it
may be said that this follower of Paul, who took hold of the
"Law–Gospel" component of Pauline thought and made it the
organizing principle of Pauline (and Christian) theology, was
thereby driven to a point where Paul's uniqueness became
imperalistic and destructive.

Other followers of Paul softened his uniqueness by bending
his insights into greater conformity with other emerging strands
of Christian faith and experience. Within the New Testament
we can observe such a "catholicizing" of Paul both in Acts and
in the Pastoral Epistles, and more subtly in Ephesians and
Colossians, and perhaps also in the very process which formed
the collection of Pauline epistles—with Ephesians perhaps
being used as an introduction.

So there he is, Paul, whose thoughts about Jews and Gentiles, law and promise, justification and wrath, proved to be
of small value to the successful statisticians of the early church.
He was rather a complication, as 2 Peter indicates so kindly:
our brother Paul who is a little hard to understand (2 Peter
3:15f.). He was honored yet pushed aside; he was the egg-
head among the operators, unique rather than universal. But
he himself thought, albeit with some arrogance, that for the
sake of Lord and the church he had to deal straightforwardly
with such issues as what had happened to the law, to that wall
of partition, now that the Messiah had come. The relationship of primitive Christianity to the law could possibly have
been avoided, glanced over, or even enthusiastically overcome
in spirituality, but Paul settled down at that wall of partition
and kept thinking about it. Poor Paul, he was a theologian, an
intellectual, and perhaps the only one in the whole first-gener-
ation church. In any case, he was the only one among the
New Testament authors who had an M. Div. or its equivalent.
Perhaps Matthew was something of an academician also, but
Paul, the purist, is plagued by his professional antecedents.
He stands out rather uniquely.

We have pointed out how this pioneering theological work

of Paul became significant in a totally new way for Augustine,
the West, and the Reformation: a mighty pattern, a mighty
analysis of the nature of our hope and its fulfillment lifted
from the pages of Paul and applied in new situations. I have
spoken rather critically of these transformations and reinterpre-
tations. Ultimately, however, I do not wish to do so, because
all this interpretation and reinterpretation is what happens and
what should happen and what will happen in the ongoing and
organic life of a church which lives with its Bible. If my
image of understanding a text in its original setting and language—thinking in a bilingual way—is correct, an ever new
translation must take place. Our study has called us to recognize that when we are involved in such interpretation, we must
remember that we should interpret the original rather than
reinterpret the later interpretations. What has happened to
Christianity is that instead of having free access to the original,
we have lived in a sort of chain reaction—Augustine touching
up Paul, and with Pelagius discussing and turning these things
around, the medievalists pushing one way or another, and then
further reactions, moving away from the original. We must
now take a fresh look at the original and try to make our own
translation, learning from the older versions and from the
Confessions, to be sure, but translating the *text* and not the
translations. The original is there, and I have tried to point
to it. The original is there, and to return to *it* is to be a true
son or daughter of the Reformation.

This "original" stands out as unique, and to allow for such
uniqueness requires a view of Scripture that can withstand the
mighty forces of homogenization. Those forces are powerful
since they have a legitimate source in the need for unity in
the Christian message and in Christian doctrine, but unity c n
be achieved by illegitimate short cuts and at too high a price.

We must remember that the church withstood exactly that
temptation when an attempt at a single harmonized gospel, the
Diatessaron (as produced by Tatian, ca. 170) was roundly
defeated and it was made clear that there should be four distinct gospels (in Semitic terms: *Evangelion da-mephareshe*, the
separated gospel). For the richness of revelation could not be

maintained if the apologetic needs for harmonization were allowed to swallow up the uniqueness of the distinct messages. This analogy is a good one and encourages us to recapture Paul in his full uniqueness.

It would be tempting to go on from here and sharpen up the ways in which Paul's insights and perspectives lead him to see dangers in the thought and the piety of others. This would perhaps especially be true in relation to the theology and piety reflected in the Gospel of John. It is not difficult, for example, to see how Paul's teaching on the resurrection in 1 Corinthians 15 is a critique not of those who deny the fact of Christ's resurrection, but of those who claim that "the resurrection has happened already" (cf. 2 Tim. 2:18, and Justin Martyr's *Dialogue with Trypho*, ch. 80). Paul's emphasis is on the fact that there are still many things that need to happen before the great and glorious general resurrection. His thinking here is consistent with his pervasive emphasis on how Christians still groan together with the creation, longing for liberation. To Paul the faith is still hoping—not having (Rom. 8:24–25). This pattern of thought and piety is for Paul part and parcel of his understanding of the weakness of the cross. It makes him ever suspicious of all triumphalism, of all overstatements concerning victory. For him even hope and faith take second place to that love by which Christians coexist in Christ with partial and obscured vision, prophecy, and knowledge (1 Cor. 13:11–13).

Perhaps it was Paul's innate arrogance, his firm convictions, that led him to see and sense the limits and pitfalls of his own attitudes. Thus he became the constant critic of triumphalism and all patterns of divinization. Or it may have been something in his Jewish heritage that prompted him to recognize that it was not good for human beings to forget their creatureliness, or to claim that the Messianic Age had come when it obviously had not—except in hope and faith. Clearly Paul is the perpetual critic of the overstatements of the faith. For that reason, God's time table and the consequent "not yet" is so important to Paul.

Johannine theology displays little or no such hesitation.

There Martha's expectation that her brother will rise on the last day is countered by Jesus' answer: "He who believes in me, though he die, yet shall he live, and whoever lives and believes in me shall never die . . ." (Jn. 11:25f.), a theological statement enforced and symbolized by the raising of Lazarus (cf. Jn. 5:24: "He who hears my word . . . *has* passed from death to life.") The Johannine passion narrative thus quite consistently sees the crucifixion of Jesus in victorious terms: he is not crucified, he is lifted up. He is glorified, he asks for water not because he is thirsty but because he knows that the Scriptures must be fulfilled, and his final word is not, as in Mark and Matthew, the cry of desolation: "My God, my God, why hast thou forsaken me?" (Mt. 27:46, Mk. 15:34). Rather, in John, he utters a cry of victory: "It is accomplished!" (Jn. 19:30).

The pattern of language—rightly identified as gnostic with a small "g"—used by John is the very language which Paul finds dangerous. In short, we do encounter the richness of New Testament diversity. It can, of course, be shown how the Johannine gospel guards itself in its own way from the most undesirable consequences of such language; and there are even good reasons to recognize how later editorial work put in further safeguards—an apt parallel to how Paul's uniqueness was checked, for example, by the Pastoral Epistles. But the main lesson for us is to recognize and rejoice in the richness of the diversity.

How, then, does the church, the Christian, the preacher, the individual Bible reader live with the richness of diversity? First, we must overcome our defensive instincts. We need not defend God or the Bible. While we may find and rejoice in themes, lessons, and concepts that seem to hold the Bible together, we should not think that such an enterprise is actually what holds it together. The unity of the Scriptures is rooted in the experience of the church which found these various ways of speaking and thinking to be authentic witnesses to the one Lord.

Second, we must recognize fully that one *can* speak, think, pray, preach in various modes, moods, and languages, be they Matthean or Lukan, Pauline or Johannine—and that all these languages have their glories *and* their risks.

Third, we will become increasingly sensitive to the simple truth that there is no *one* universal "biblical" or even "New Testament" language. Rather, we will recognize that the clarity, integrity, and power of the message is available to us only in the uniqueness of each of these distinct theologies. For the intention of an author like Paul is often found at the point where he differs from the others, where he feels that the understanding of others leads to harmful attitudes and distortions of the faith.

Fourth, we must ask—seriously, not just rhetorically—whether the issues to which Paul speaks apply to our situations, our predicaments. The answer could at times be negative—for it is reasonable to expect that our questions could be different ones. After all, he seems to speak quite differently to different churches. We cannot take for granted that he would answer us as he answered the Corinthians *and* the Galatians *and* the Thessalonians. It is even possible that we could be in a situation where the Pauline warnings against triumphalism—while most important—would just feed into a morbid self-flagellation or a mood of sour grapes defeatism and that what *we* need is the powerful and exuberant fugues of Johannine theology.

The uniqueness present in the catholic totality of the Scriptures thus requires a careful analysis of whether our situation is analogous and similar to the one addressed by a biblical text. Martin Luther was sensitive to this question. When some people quoted Scripture to him, he could say: Yes, it is the word of God—but I do not think that it is the word of God to me. Jesus could say: "Those who are not against us are for us" and "He who is not for me is against me." But these things are not to be said at the same time, not to the same people. They answer distinctly different questions.

****

These chapters have been written out of an ever growing fascination with and admiration for the Apostle Paul. His perspective and perception, his grasp and sensitivity, have become very dear to me. The more I have seen his uniqueness, the more I have recognized his limitations. Limitation is the twin of uniqueness. When I see Paul's limitations, his arrogance, his difficulties in carrying out the implications of even his most penetrating insights—e.g. in the matter of slaves and women—his greatness has not thereby been diminished, it has only become more real. He remains a great theologian—with his own special flaws. I am happy to find his epistles within a New Testament where, in his uniqueness, he is only one among others who attempted to proclaim the gospel and its consequences. Some of the others who wrote for the New Testament may well be inferior to Paul in intellectual power, but richly compensated by the Spirit and by common sense—less prone to elitism. For, as Origen so rightly said to that snob Celsus when he criticized Christianity for not being up to academic standards: "We cook for the common people."

The original writings of Paul in all their uniqueness are indispensable to the Christian community as they picture his call to be our champion, a Jew who by vicarious penetration gives to us Gentiles the justification for our claims to be God's children in Jesus Christ. In an odd and implicit manner, his writings put questions to our preoccupation with our egos and our feelings, for he writes about justification rather than forgiveness. And his deep insight into the role of weakness in the life of religious people remains equally indispensable for all Christians.

Thus it may be right to end this study of Paul with the observation that the work and thought of Paul would have been lost had not his unique mission been a part of that wider and diverse Jesus movement into which he came in a unique manner. He came by God's call of a Jew, justifying the right of us Gentiles by a unique argument of faith. He was creatively puzzled by his own weakness, and attempting to learn the lesson of love as he found limitations in his own ability to persuade others to think as he did.

We may be allowed to guess that Paul would be willing to be only one of many, unique, incapable of being universal without the help of others. Thus he rests well in the midst of others found among the books of the New Testament. There we see him in his indispensable uniqueness.

THE APOSTLE PAUL AND THE
INTROSPECTIVE CONSCIENCE OF THE WEST*

Dedicated to Henry J. Cadbury (1883–1974)
on his eightieth birthday.

In the history of Western Christianity—and hence, to a large extent, in the history of Western culture—the Apostle Paul has been hailed as a hero of the introspective conscience. Here was the man who grappled with the problem "I do not do the good I want, but the evil I do not want to do is what I do . . ." (Rom. 7:19). His insights as to a solution of this dilemma have recently been more or less identified, for example, with what Jung referred to as the Individuation Process;[1] but this

* This paper was delivered as the invited Address at the Annual Meeting of the American Psychological Association, September 3, 1961; it is a revised and footnoted edition of my article "Paulus och Samvetet," published in Sweden in *Svensk Exegetisk Arsbok* 25 (1960), 62–77. In its present form the essay appeared in the *Harvard Theological Review*, 56 (1963), 199–215, and is reprinted with the permission of that journal.
It is with some hesitation that I burden the reader with this article. Not that I do not believe in what it says. I do, and I even consider it important. But the reader will find that it repeats some of the things covered in the preceding essay. On the other hand, it is the original statement of the perspective on Paul from which we have seen Paul among Jews and Gentiles. It could serve well both as a summary and as a more concise statement of what is at stake in our attempt to renew our acquaintance with Paul after nineteen hundred years. I apologize for the repetitiousness and take refuge in the often true adage: repetition is the mother of learning. I also welcome the opportunity of answering the severe criticism that Professor Ernst Käsemann of Tübingen leveled against this article, see below, pp. 129–33.
1. D. Cox. *Jung and St. Paul: A Study of the Doctrine of Justification by Faith and Its Relation to the Concept of Individuation* (1959).—Attention should also be drawn to the discussion in *The American Psychologist* (1960), 301–4, 713–16, initiated by O. H. Mower's article " 'Sin,' the Lesser of Two Evils"; cf. also the Symposium of W. H. Clark, O. H. Mowrer, A. Ellis, Ch. Curran and E. J. Shoben, Jr., on "The Role of the Concept of Sin in Psycho-

is only a contemporary twist to the traditional Western way of reading the Pauline letters as documents of human consciousness.

Twenty-five years ago Henry J. Cadbury wrote a stimulating study, "The Peril of Modernizing Jesus" (1937). That book and that very title is a good summary of one of the most important insights of biblical studies in the 20th century. It has ramifications far beyond the field of theology and biblical exegesis. It questions the often tacit presupposition that man remains basically the same through the ages. There is little point in affirming or denying such a presupposition in general terms—much would depend on what the foggy word "basically" could mean. But both the historian and the theologian, both the psychologist and the average reader of the Bible, are well advised to assess how this hypothesis of contemporaneity affects their thinking, and their interpretation of ancient writings.

This problem becomes acute when one tries to picture the function and the manifestation of introspection in the life and writings of the Apostle Paul. It is the more acute since it is exactly at this point that Western interpreters have found the common denominator between Paul and the experience of man, since Paul's statements about "justification by faith" have been hailed as the answer to the problem which faces the ruthlessly honest man in his practice of introspection. Especially in Protestant Christianity—which, however, at this point has its roots in Augustine and in the piety of the Middle Ages —the Pauline awareness of sin has been interpreted in the light of Luther's struggle with his conscience. But it is exactly at that point that we can discern the most drastic difference between Luther and Paul, between the 16th and the 1st century, and, perhaps, between Eastern and Western Christianity.

---

therapy," *Journal of Counseling Psychology* 7 (1960), 185–201.—For an unusually perceptive and careful attempt to deal with historical material from a psychoanalytical point of view, see Erik H. Erikson, *Young Man Luther* (1958). Not only the abundance but also the "Western" nature of the Luther material makes such an attempt more reasonable than when it is applied to Paul, who, as Erikson remarks, remains "in the twilight of biblical psychology" (p. 94).

A fresh look at the Pauline writings themselves shows that Paul was equipped with what in our eyes must be called a rather "robust" conscience.[2] In Phil. 3 Paul speaks most fully about his life before his Christian calling, and there is no indication that he had had any difficulty in fulfilling the Law. On the contrary, he can say that he had been "flawless" as to the righteousness required by the Law (v.6). His encounter with Jesus Christ—at Damascus, according to Acts 9:1–9—has not changed this fact. It was not to him a restoration of a plagued conscience; when he says that he now forgets what is behind him (Phil. 3:13), he does not think about the shortcomings in his obedience to the Law, but about his glorious achievements as a righteous Jew, achievements which he nevertheless now has learned to consider as "refuse" in the light of his faith in Jesus as the Messiah.

The impossibility of keeping the whole Law is a decisive point in Paul's argumentation in Rom. 2:17—3:20 (cf. 2:1ff.); and also in Gal. 3:10–12 this impossibility is the background for Paul's arguments in favor of a salvation which is open to both Jews and Gentiles in Christ. These and similar Pauline statements have led many interpreters to accuse Paul of misunderstanding or deliberately distorting the Jewish view of Law and Salvation.[3] It is pointed out that for the Jew the Law did not require a static or pedantic perfectionism but supposed a covenant relationship in which there was room for forgiveness and repentance and where God applied the Meas-

---

2. The actual meaning of the Greek word *syneidesis*, usually translated "conscience," is a complex linguistic problem, see C. A. Pierce, *Conscience in The New Testament* (1955).—The more general problem dealt with in this lecture is closer to the problem to which P. Althaus draws attention in his *Paulus und Luther über den Menschen* (1951), cf. the critique by F. Büchsel, *Theologische Blätter* 17 (1938), 306–11.—B. Reicke, *The Disobedient Spirits and Christian Baptism* (1946), 174–82, gives the meaning "loyalty" in 1 Peter 3:21, cf. idem, "Syneidesis in Röm. 2:15," *Theologische Zeitschrift* 12 (1956), 157–61.—See also C. Spicq, *Revue Biblique* 47 (1938), 50–80, and J. Dupont, *Studia Hellenistica* 5 (1948), 119–53.

3. See esp. G. F. Moore, *Judaism*, vol. III (1930), 151.—H. J. Schoeps, *Paul* (1961), 213–18, voices the same criticism from the anachronistic point of modern Old Testament interpretation as carried out by M. Buber and others. Cf., however, M. Buber, *Two Types of Faith* (1951), 46–50.

ure of Grace. Hence Paul should have been wrong in ruling out the Law on the basis that Israel could not achieve the perfect obedience which the Law required. What is forgotten in such a critique of Paul—which is conditioned by the later Western problem of a conscience troubled by the demands of the Law—is that these statements about the impossibility of fulfilling the Law stand side by side with the one just mentioned: "I was blameless as to righteousness—of the Law, that is" (Phil. 3:6). So Paul speaks about his subjective conscience—in full accordance with his Jewish training. But Rom. 2—3 deals with someting very different. The actual transgressions in Israel—as a people, not in each and every individual—show that the Jews are not better than the Gentiles, in spite of circumcision and the proud possession of the Law. The "advantage" of the Jews is that they have been entrusted with the Words of God and this advantage cannot be revoked by their disobedience (Rom. 3:1ff.), but for the rest they have no edge on salvation. The Law has not helped. They stand before God as guilty as the Gentiles, and even more so (2:9). All this is said in the light of the new avenue of salvation, which has been opened in Christ, an avenue which is equally open to Jews and Gentiles, since it is not based on the Law, in which the very distinction between the two rests. In such a situation, says Paul, the old covenant, even with its provision for forgiveness and grace, is not a valid alternative any more. The only *metanoia* (repentance/conversion) and the only grace which counts is the one now available in Messiah Jesus. Once this has been seen, it appears that Paul's references to the impossibility of fulfilling the Law is part of a theological and theoretical scriptural argument about the relation between Jews and Gentiles. Judging from Paul's own writings, there is no indication that he had "experienced it in his own conscience" during his time as a Pharisee. It is also striking to note that Paul never urges Jews to find in Christ the answer to the anguish of a plagued conscience.

If that is the case regarding *Paul the Pharisee*, it is, as we shall see, even more important to note that we look in vain for any evidence that *Paul the Christian* has suffered under the burden of conscience concerning personal shortcomings which he would label "sins." The famous formula "simul justus et peccator"—at the same time righteous and sinner—as a description of the status of the Christian may have some foundation in the Pauline writings, but this formula cannot be substantiated as the center of Paul's conscious attitude toward his personal sins. Apparently, Paul did not have the type of introspective conscience which such a formula seems to presuppose.[4] This is probably one of the reasons why "forgiveness" is the term for salvation which is used least of all in the Pauline writings.[5]

It is most helpful to compare these observations concerning Paul with the great hero of what has been called "Pauline Christianity," i.e., with Martin Luther. In him we find the problem of late medieval piety and theology. Luther's inner struggles presuppose the developed system of Penance and Indulgence, and it is significant that his famous 95 theses take their point of departure from the problem of forgiveness of sins as seen within the framework of Penance: "When our Lord and Master Jesus Christ said: 'Repent (*penitentiam agite*) . . . ,' he wanted the whole life of the faithful to be a repentance (or: penance)."

When the period of the European mission had come to an end, the theological and practical center of Penance shifted from Baptism, administered once and for all, to the ever repeated Mass, and already this subtle change in the architecture

---

4. For a penetrating analysis of the original meaning of this formula in Luther's theology, and its relation to the Pauline writings, see W. Joest, "Paulus und das lutherische Simul Justus et Peccator," *Kerygma und Dogma* I (1956), 270–321.—See also R. Bring, "Die paulinische Begründung der lutherischen Theologie," *Luthertum* 17 (1955), 18–43; and *idem, Commentary on Galatians* (1961); H. Pohlmann, "Hat Luther Paulus entdeckt?" *Studien der Luther-Akademie* N. F. 7 (1949).—For a perceptive view of the role of Luther's conscience, see A. Siirala, *Gottes Gebot bei Martin Luther* (1956), 282 ff.

5. There is actually no use of the term in the undisputed Pauline epistles; it is found as an apposition in Eph. 1:7 and Col. 1:14; cf. the O. T. quotation in Rom. 4:7, where Paul's own preference for "justification" is clear from the context, and the similar term "remission" in Rom. 3:25.—Cf. my articles "Sünde und Schuld" and "Sündenvergebung," Die Religion in Geschichte und Gegenwart, vol. 6 (1962), 484–89, and 511–13, with a discussion of the absence of a common word for "guilt."

of the Christian life contributed to a more acute introspection.[6] The manuals for self-examination among the Irish monks and missionaries became a treasured legacy in wide circles of Western Christianity. The Black Death may have been significant in the development of the climate of faith and life. Penetrating self-examination reached a hitherto unknown intensity. For those who took this practice seriously—and they were more numerous than many Protestants are accustomed to think —the pressure was great. It is as one of those—and for them —that Luther carries out his mission as a great pioneer. It is in response to *their* question, "How can I find a gracious God?" that Paul's words about a justification in Christ by faith, and without the works of the Law, appears as the liberating and saving answer. Luther's unrelenting honesty, even to the gates of hell (cf. especially his *De servo arbitrio*, "On the Bondage of the Will"), his refusal to accept the wise and sound consolation from his spiritual directors, these make him into a Christopher Columbus in the world of faith, who finds new and good land on the other side of what was thought to be the abyss.

In these matters Luther was a truly Augustinian monk, since Augustine may well have been one of the first to express the dilemma of the introspective conscience. It has always been a puzzling fact that Paul meant so relatively little for the thinking of the Church during the first 350 years of its history. To be sure, he is honored and quoted but—in the theological perspective of the West—it seems that Paul's great insight into justification by faith was forgotten.[7] It is, however, with

6. For this change and its effect on Christology, see G. H. Williams, "The Sacramental Presuppositions of Anselm's Cur deus homo," *Church History* 26 (1957), 245–74.

7. For early Pauline interpretation see K. Staab, *Pauluskommentare aus der griechischen Kirche* (1933); V. E. Hasler, *Gesetz und Evangelium in der alten Kirche bis Origenes* (1953); E. Aleith, *Paulusverständnis in der alten Kirche* (1937); P. G. Verweijs, *Evangelium und Gesetz in der ältesten Christenheit bis auf Marcion* (1960); now also U. Wickert, "Die Persönlichkeit des Paulus in den Paulus kommentaren Theodors von Mopsuestia," *Zeitschrift für die neutestamentliche Wissenschaft* 53 (1962), 51–66. For Paul and conscience in relation to Gnosticism, see F. F. Sagnard, *Clément d'Alexandrie, Extraits de Théodote* (1948), 247–49, and R. M. Grant's observations in *Journal of Theological Studies* 7 (1956), 310 f.

Augustine that we find an interpretation of Paul which makes use of what to us is the deeper layer in the thought of the great Apostle. A decisive reason for this state of affairs may well have been that up to the time of Augustine the Church was by and large under the impression that Paul dealt with those issues with which he actually deals: 1) What happens to the Law (the Torah, the actual Law of Moses, not the principle of legalism) when the Messiah has come?[8] 2) What are the ramifications of the Messiah's arrival for the relation between Jews and Gentiles? For Paul had not arrived at his view of the Law by testing and pondering its effect upon his conscience; it was his grappling with the question about the place of the Gentiles in the Church and in the plan of God, with the problem Jews/Gentiles or Jewish Christians/Gentile Christians,[9] which had driven him to that interpretation of the Law which was to become his in a unique way.[10] These observations agree well with the manner in which both Paul himself and the Acts of the Apostles describe his "conversion" as a call to become the Apostle to and for the Gentiles. This was the task for which he—in the manner of the prophets of old—had been earmarked by God from his mother's womb (Gal. 1:15, cf. Acts 9:15).[11] There is not—as we usually think—

8. For the Jewish background to this problem as the one relevant to Paul, see W. D. Davies, *Torah in the Messianic Age and/or the Age to Come* (1952); also H. J. Schoeps, *op. cit.*, 174, with reference to the talmudic tractate Sanhedrin 98a.

9. It is significant that the contrast in Paul is between Jews and Gentiles, or Jewish Christians and Gentile Christians, but never between Jews and Gentile Christians; see G. Bornkamm, "Gesetz und Natur: Röm 2:14–16," *Studien zu Antike und Urchristentum* (1959), 93–118; cf. J. N. Sevenster, *Paul and Seneca* (1961), 96. [In the light of Rom. 11:11–36, I would now question Bornkamm's view.]

10. A. Schweitzer was certainly right when he recognized that Paul's teaching about justification by faith had such a limited function in Paul's theology and could not be considered the center of his total view. "The doctrine of righteousness by faith is therefore a subsidiary crater. . . ." *The Mysticism of Paul the Apostle* (1931), 225. [Schweitzer's view of what is the "main crater" is, however, quite different from mine.]

11. J. Munck, *Paul and the Salvation of Mankind* (1959), ch. 1; see also H. G. Wood, "The Conversion of St. Paul. Its Nature, Antecedents and Consequences," *New Testament Studies* 1 (1954/55), 276–82; and U. Wilckens, "Die Bekehrung des Paulus als religionsgeschichtliches Problem," *Zeitschrift für Theologie und Kirche* 56 (1959), 273–93.

first a conversion, and then a call to apostleship; there is only the call to the work among the Gentiles. Hence, it is quite natural that at least one of the centers of gravity in Paul's thought should be how to define the place for Gentiles in the Church, according to the plan of God. Rom. 9—11 is not an appendix to chs. 1—8, but the climax of the letter.

This problem was, however, not a live one after the end of the first century, when Christianity for all practical purposes had a non-Jewish constituency. Yet it was not until Augustine that the Pauline thought about the Law and Justification was applied in a consistent and grand style to a more general and timeless human problem. In that connection we remember that Augustine has often been called "the first modern man." While this is an obvious generalization, it may contain a fair amount of truth. His *Confessions* is the first great document in the history of the introspective conscience. The Augustinian line leads into the Middle Ages and reaches its climax in the penitential struggle of an Augustinian monk, Martin Luther, and in his interpretation of Paul.[12]

Judging at least from a superficial survey of the preaching of the Churches of the East from olden times to the present, it is striking how their homiletical tradition is either one of doxology or meditative mysticism or exhortation—but it does not deal with the plagued conscience in the way in which one came to do so in the Western Churches.

The problem we are trying to isolate could be expressed in hermeneutical terms somewhat like this: The Reformers' interpretation of Paul rests on an analogism when Pauline statements about Faith and Works, Law and Gospel, Jews and

---

12. For the Augustinian interpretation see A. F. W. Lekkerkerker, *Römer 7 und Römer 9 bei Augustin* (1942); cf. Ph. Platz, "Der Römerbrief in der Gnadenlehre Augustins," *Cassiciacum 5* (1938); also J. Stelzenberger, *Conscientia bei Augustin* (1959); and *idem*, "Conscientia in der ost-westlichen Spannung der patristischen Theologie," *Tübinger Theologische Quartalschrift* 141 (1961), 174–205.—For the Greek background, see O. Seel, "Zur Vorgeschichte des Gewissensbegriffes im altgriechischen Denken," *Festschrift F. Dornseiff* (1953), 291–319. For a broad and instructive survey, which substantiates our view in many respects—but reads the biblical material differently—see H. Jaeger, "L'examen de conscience dans les religions non-chrétiennes et avant le christianisme," *Numen 6* (1959), 175–233.

Gentiles are read in the framework of late medieval piety. The Law, the Torah, with its specific requirements of circumcision and food restrictions becomes a general principle of "legalism" in religious matters. Where Paul was concerned about the possibility for Gentiles to be included in the messianic community, his statements are now read as answers to the quest for assurance about man's salvation out of a common human predicament.

This shift in the frame of reference affects the interpretation at many points. A good illustration can be seen in what Luther calls the Second Use of the Law, i.e., its function as a Tutor or Schoolmaster unto Christ. The crucial passage for this understanding of the Law is Gal. 3:24, a passage which the King James Version—in unconscious accord with Western tradition—renders: "Wherefore the law was our schoolmaster (RV and ASV.: tutor) to bring us unto Christ," but which the Revised Standard Version translates more adequately: "So that the law was our custodian until Christ came."[12a] In his extensive argument for the possibility of Gentiles becoming Christians without circumcision etc., Paul states that the Law had not come in until 430 years after the promise to Abraham, and that it was meant to have validity only up to the time of the Messiah (Gal. 3:15–22). Hence, its function was to serve as a Custodian for the Jews until that time. Once the Messiah had come, and once the faith in Him—not "faith" as a general religious attitude—was available as the decisive ground for salvation, the Law had done its duty as a custodian for the Jews, or as a waiting room with strong locks (vv. 22f.). Hence, it is clear that Paul's problem is how to explain why there is no reason to impose the Law on the Gentiles, who now, in God's good Messianic time, have become partakers in the fulfillment of the promises to Abraham (v.29).

In the common interpretation of Western Christianity, the matter looks very different. One could even say that Paul's argument has been reversed into saying the opposite to his

---

12a. Cf. my article on Gal. 3:24 in *Svensk Exegetisk Årsbok* 18–19 (1953–54), 161–73.

original intention. Now the Law is the Tutor *unto* Christ. Nobody can attain a true faith in Christ unless his self-righteousness has been crushed by the Law . The function of the Second Use of the Law is to make man see his desperate need for a Savior. In such an interpretation, we note how Paul's distinction between Jews and Gentiles is gone. "Our Tutor/ Custodian" is now a statement applied to man in general, not "our" in the sense of "I, Paul, and my fellow Jews." Furthermore, the Law is not any more the Law of Moses which requires circumcision etc., and which has become obsolete when faith in the Messiah is a live option—it is the moral imperative as such, in the form of the will of God. And finally, Paul's argument that the Gentiles must not, and should not come to Christ *via* the Law, i.e., *via* circumcision etc., has turned into a statement according to which all men must come to Christ with consciences properly convicted by the Law and its insatiable requirements for righteousness. So drastic is the reinterpretation once the original framework of "Jews and Gentiles" is lost, and the Western problems of conscience become its unchallenged and self-evident substitute.

Thus, the radical difference between a Paul and a Luther at this one point has considerable ramification for the reading of the actual texts. And the line of Luther appears to be the obvious one. This is true not only among those who find themselves more or less dogmatically bound by the confessions of the Reformation. It is equally true about the average student of "all the great books" in a College course, or the agnostic Westerner in general. It is also true in serious New Testament exegesis. Thus, R. Bultmann—in spite of his great familiarity with the history of religions in early Christian times—finds the nucleus of Pauline thought in the problem of "boasting,"[13] i.e., in man's need to be utterly convicted in his conscience.[14] Paul's self-understanding in these matters is the existential,

13. R. Bultmann, *Theology of the New Testament*, vol. 1 (1951), 242 f.
14. C. H. Dodd feels the difficulty in such an interpretation, but ends up with placing Paul's overcoming of his boasting somewhat later in his career, "The Mind of Paul," *New Testament Studies* (1953), 67–128.

and hence, ever valid center of Pauline theology. Such an interpretation is an even more drastic translation and an even more far-reaching generalization of the original Pauline material than that found in the Reformers. But it is worth noting that it is achieved in the prolongation of the same line. This is more obvious since Bultmann makes, candidly and openly, the statement that his existential heremeneutic rests on the presupposition that man is essentially the same through the ages, and that this continuity in the human self-consciousness is the common denominator between the New Testament and any age of human history. This presupposition is stated with the force of an a priori truth.[15]

What in Bultmann rests on a clearly stated heremeneutic principle plays, however, its subtle and distorting role in historians who do not give account of their presuppositions but work within an unquestioned Western framework. P. Volz, in his comprehensive study of Jewish eschatology, uses man's knowledge of his individual salvation in its relation to a troubled conscience as one of the "trenches" in his reconstruction of the Jewish background to the New Testament.[16] But when it comes to the crucial question and he wants to find a passage which could substantiate that this was a conscious problem in those generations of Judaism, he can find only one example in the whole Rabbinic literature which perhaps could illustrate an attitude of a troubled conscience (bBer. 28b).[17]

To be sure, no one could ever deny that hamartia, "sin," is a crucial word in Paul's terminology, especially in his epistle to the Romans. Rom 1—3 sets out to show that all—both Jews

15. Bultmann, ibm. vol. 2 (1955) 251; cf. idem, "The Problem of Hermeneutics," Essays Philosophical and Theological (1955), 234–61.

16. Volz, Die Eschatologie der jüdischen Gemeinde im neutestamentlichen Zeitalter (1934), 111 ff.

17. Cf. also how F. Büchsel, who repeats this view in highly biased language, admits the lack of evidence for such an attitude: the Pharisee "tended to vacillate between an arrogant confidence in his good works, which blinded him to his sinfulness, and a hopeless fear of God's wrath, though this is more rarely expressed." Theological Dictionary of the New Testament (Ed. G. Kittel), vol. 3 (1965), 935.—The examples, often quoted, from 4 Ezra 3—4 and 7—8 deal primarily with the historical theodicy and not with the individual conscience.

and Gentiles—have sinned and fallen short of the Glory of God
(3:19, cf. v. 23). Rom. 3:21—8:39 demonstrates how and in
what sense this tragic fact is changed by the arrival of the
Messiah.

It is much harder to gage how Paul subjectively experienced
the power of sin in his life and, more specifically, how and in
what sense he was conscious of actual sins. One point is clear.
The Sin with capital S in Paul's past was that he had persecuted the Church of God. This climax of his dedicated
obedience to his Jewish faith (Gal. 1:13, Phil. 3:6) was the
shameful deed which made him the least worthy of apostleship
(1 Cor. 15:9). This motif, which is elaborated dramatically
by the author of the Acts of the Apostles (chs. 9, 22 and 26),
is well grounded in Paul's own epistles. Similarly, when
1 Timothy states on Paul's account that "Christ Jesus came into
the world to save sinners, of whom I am number one" (1:15),
this is not an expression of contrition in the present tense, but
refers to how Paul in his ignorance had been a blaspheming and
violent persecutor, before God in his mercy and grace had revealed to him his true Messiah and made Paul an Apostle and
a prototype of sinners' salvation (1:12–16).[18]

Nevertheless, Paul knew that he had made up for this terrible Sin of persecuting the Church, as he says in so many words
in 1 Cor. 15:10: ". . . his grace toward me was not in vain;
on the contrary, I worked harder than any of them—though it
was not I, but the grace of God which is with me."

Thus his call to Apostleship has the same pattern as the more
thematic statement that Christ died for us godless ones, while
we were yet sinners (Rom. 5:6–11). We note how that
statement is only the subsidiary conditional clause in an argument *e majore ad minus*: If now God was so good and powerful that he could justify weak and sinful and rebellious men,
how much easier must it not be for him to give in due time the
ultimate salvation to those whom he already has justified.

---

18. This theme is elaborated further in the Epistle of Barnabas 5:9, where *all*
the Apostles are called "iniquitous above all sin," with a reference to Mk. 2:17.

Hence, the words about the sinful, the weak and the rebellious have not present tense meaning, but refer to the past, which is gloriously and gracefully blotted out, as was Paul's enmity to Jesus Christ and his Church.

What then about Paul's consciousness of sins after his conversion? His letters indicate with great clarity that he did not hold to the view that man was free from sin after baptism. His pastoral admonitions show that he had much patience with the sins and weaknessess of Christians. But does he ever intimate that he is aware of any sins of his own which would trouble his conscience? It is actually easier to find statements to the contrary. The tone in Acts 23:1, "Brethren, I have lived before God in all good conscience up to this day" (cf. 24:16), prevails also throughout his letters. Even if we take due note of the fact that the major part of Paul's correspondence contains an apology for his Apostolic ministry—hence it is the antipode to Augustine's *Confessions* from the point of view of form—the conspicuous absence of references to an actual consciousness of being a sinner is surprising. To be sure, Paul is aware of a struggle with his "body" (1 Cor. 9:27), but we note that the tone is one of confidence, not of a plagued conscience.

In Rom. 9:1 and 2 Cor. 1:12 he witnesses to his good conscience. This tone reaches its highest pitch in 2 Cor. 5:10f.: "For we must all appear before the judgment seat of Christ so that each one may receive the retribution for what he has done while in his body, either good or evil. Aware, therefore, of the fear of the Lord, we try to persuade men, but to God it is clear [what we are]; and I hope that it is clear also to your conscience." Here, with the day of reckoning before his eyes, Paul says that the Lord has approved of him, and he hopes that the Corinthians shall have an equally positive impression of him, and of his success in pleasing the Lord (5:9). This robust conscience is not shaken but strengthened by his awareness of a final judgment which has not come yet. And when he writes about the tensions between himself and Apollos and other teachers, he states that "I have nothing on my conscience" (1 Cor. 4:4; NEB—literally "I know nothing with me"; the verb is of the same stem as the word for conscience); to be sure, he adds that this does not settle the case, since "the Lord is my judge," but it is clear from the context that Paul is in little doubt about the final verdict. His warning against a premature verdict is not a plea out of humility or fear, but a plea to the Corinthians not to be too rash in a negative evaluation of Paul.

Thus, we look in vain for a statement in which Paul would speak about himself as an actual sinner. When he speaks about his conscience, he witnesses to his good conscience before men and God. On the other hand, Paul often speaks about his *weakness*, not only ironically as in 2 Cor. 11:21f. In 2 Cor. 12 we find the proudly humble words, "But He said to me: 'My grace is sufficient to you, for the power is fulfilled in weakness.' I will the more gladly boast of my weakness, that the power of Christ may rest upon me. For the sake of Christ, then, I am content with weaknesses, insults, hardships, persecutions, and calamities; for when I am weak, then I am strong" (vv. 9–10). The weakness which Paul here refers to is clearly without any relation to his sin or his conscience. The "thorn in the flesh" (v. 7) was presumably some physical handicap— some have guessed at epilepsy—which interfered with his effectiveness and, what was more important, with his apostolic authority, as we can see from Gal. 4:13, cf. 1. Cor. 11:30. Sickness was seen as a sign of insufficient spiritual endowment. But there is no indication that Paul ever thought of this and other "weaknesses" as sins for which he was responsible. They were caused by the Enemy or the enemies. His weakness became for him an important facet in his identification with the work of Christ, who had been "crucified in weakness" (2 Cor. 13:4; cf. also 4:10 and Col. 1:24).—In the passage from Rom. 5, mentioned above, we find the only use of the word "weak" as a synonym to "sinner," but there these words helped to describe primarily the power of justification as a past act (and the New English Bible consequently renders it by "powerless"). This is the more clear since the third synonym is "enemy" (v. 10), and points to Paul's past when he had been the enemy of Christ.

Yet there is one Pauline text which the reader must have wondered why we have left unconsidered, especially since it is the passage we mentioned in the begining as the proof text for Paul's deep insights into the human predicament: "I do not do the good I want, but the evil I do not want to do is what I do" (Rom. 7:19). What could witness more directly to a deep and sensitive introspective conscience? While much attention has been given to the question whether Paul here speaks about a pre-Christian or Christian experience of his, or about man in general, little attention has been drawn to the fact that Paul here is involved in an argument about the Law; he is not primarily concerned about man's or his own cloven ego or predicament.[19] The diatribe style of the chapter helps us to see what Paul is doing. In vv. 7–12 he works out an answer to the semi-rhetorical question: "Is the Law sin?" The answer reads: "Thus the Law is holy, just, and good." This leads to the equally rhetorical question: "Is it then this good (Law) which brought death to me?", and the answer is summarized in v. 25b: "So then, I myself serve the Law of God with my mind, but with my flesh I serve the Law of Sin" (i.e., the Law "weakened by sin" [8:3] leads to death, just as a medicine which is good in itself can cause death to a patient whose organism [flesh] cannot take it).

Such an analysis of the formal structure of Rom. 7 shows that Paul is here involved in an interpretation of the Law, a defense for the holiness and goodness of the Law. In vv. 13–25 he carries out this defense by making a distinction between the Law as such and the Sin (and the Flesh) which has to assume the whole responsibility for the fatal outcome. It is most striking that the "I," the *ego*, is not simply identified with Sin and Flesh. The observation that "I do not do the good I want, but the evil I do not want to do is what I do"

---

19. The confusion caused by psychological interpretations, and the centrality of the Law in Rom. 7, was seen in the epoch–making study by W. G. Kümmel, *Römer 7 und die Bekehrung des Paulus* (1929); cf. C. L. Mitton, *Expository Times* 65 (1953/54), 78–81; 99–103; 132–135; and E. Ellwein, *Kerygma und Dogma* 1 (1955), 247–68.

does not lead directly over to the exclamation: "Wretched man that I am . . . !", but, on the contrary, to the statement, "Now if I do what I do not want, *then it is not I who do it*, but the sin which dwells in me." The argument is one of acquittal of the ego, not one of utter contrition. Such a line of thought would be impossible if Paul's intention were to describe man's predicament. In Rom. 1–3 the human impasse has been argued, and here every possible excuse has been carefully ruled out. In Rom. 7 the issue is rather to show how in some sense "I gladly agree with the Law of God as far as my inner man is concerned" (v. 11); or, as in v. 25, "I serve the Law of God."

All this makes sense only if the anthropological references in Rom. 7 are seen as means for a very special argument about the holiness and goodness of the Law. The possibility of a distinction between the good Law and the bad Sin is based on the rather trivial observation that every man knows that there is a difference between what he ought to do and what he does. This distinction makes it possible for Paul to blame Sin and Flesh, and to rescue the Law as a good gift of God. "If I now do what I do not want, I agree with the Law [and recognize] that it is good" (v. 16). That is all, but that is what should be proven.

Unfortunately—or fortunately—Paul happened to express this supporting argument so well that what to him and his contemporaries was a common sense observation appeared to later interpreters to be a most penetrating insight into the nature of man and into the nature of sin. This could happen easily once the problem about the nature and intention of God's Law was not any more as relevant a problem in the sense in which Paul grappled with it. The question about the Law became the incidental framework around the golden truth of Pauline anthropology. This is what happens when one approaches Paul with the Western question of an introspective conscience. This Western interpretation reaches its climax when it appears that even, or especially, the will of man is the center of depravation. And yet, in Rom. 7 Paul had said about that will: "The will (to do the good) is there . . ." (v. 18).

What we have called the Western interpretation has left its mark even in the field of textual reconstruction in this chapter in Romans. In Moffatt's translation of the New Testament the climax of the whole argument about the Law (v. 25b, see above) is placed before the words "wretched man that I am . . ." Such a rearrangement—without any basis in the manuscripts[20]—wants to make this exclamation the dramatic climax of the whole chapter, so that it is quite clear to the reader that Paul here gives the answer to the great problem of human existence. But by such arrangements the structure of Paul's argumentation is destroyed. What was a digression is elevated to the main factor. It should not be denied that Paul is deeply aware of the precarious situation of man in this world, where even the holy Law of God does not *help*—it actually leads to death. Hence his outburst. But there is no indication that this awareness is related to a subjective conscience struggle. If that were the case, he would have spoken of the "body of sin," but he says "body of death" (v. 25; cf. 1 Cor. 15:56). What dominates this chapter is a theological concern and the awareness that there is a positive solution available here and now by the Holy Spirit about which he speaks in ch. 8. We should not read a trembling introspective conscience into a text which is so anxious to put the blame on Sin, and that in such a way that not only the law but the will and mind of man are declared good and are found to be on the side of God.

We may have wasted too much time in trying to demonstrate a fact well known in human history—and especially in the history of religions: that sayings which originally meant one thing later on were interpreted to mean something else, something which was felt to be more relevant to human conditions of later times.

And yet, if our analysis is on the whole correct, it points to a major question in the history of mankind. We should ven-

---

20. In a similar fashion even the standard Greek text of the New Testament (the Nestle edition) indicates that ch. 7 should end with the exclamation in v. 25a, and ch. 8 begin already with v. 25b. But the New English Bible retains v. 25b as the concluding sentence in ch. 7.

ture to suggest that the West for centuries has wrongly sur-
mised that the biblical writers were grappling with problems
which no doubt are ours, but which never entered their consciousness.

For the historian this is of great significance. It could of
course always be argued that these ancients unconsciously were
up against the same problems as we are—man being the same
through the ages. But the historian is rightly anxious to stress
the value of having an adequate picture of what these people
actually thought that they were saying. He will always be
suspicious of any "modernizing," whether it be for apologetic,
doctrinal, or psychological purposes.

The theologian would be quite willing to accept and appreciate the obvious deepening of religious and human insight
which has taken place in Western thought, and which reached
a theological climax with Luther—and a secular climax with
Freud. He could perhaps argue that this Western interpretation and transformation of Pauline thought is a valid and glorious process of theological development. He could even claim
that such a development was fostered by elements implicit in
the New Testament, and especially in Paul.

The framework of "Sacred History" which we have found
to be that of Pauline theology (cf. our comments on Gal. 3:24
above) opens up a new perspective for systematic theology and
practical theology. The Pauline *ephapax* ("once for all",
Rom. 6:10) cannot be translated fully and only into something
repeated in the life of every individual believer. For Gentiles
the Law is not the Schoolmaster who leads to Christ; or it is
that only by analogy and a secondary one at that. We find
ourselves in the new situation where the faith in the Messiah
Jesus gives us the right to be called Children of God (1 Jn.
3:1). By way of analogy, one could of course say that in some
sense every man has a "legalistic Jew" in his heart. But that
is an analogy, and should not be smuggled into the texts as
their primary or explicit meaning in Paul. If that is done,
something happens to the joy and humility of Gentile Christianity.

Thus, the theologian would note that the Pauline original

should not be identified with such interpretations. He would try to find ways by which the church—also in the West—could do more justice to other elements of the Pauline original than those catering to the problems raised by introspection. He would be suspicious of a teaching and a preaching which pretended that the only door into the church was that of evermore introspective awareness of sin and guilt. For it appears that the Apostle Paul was a rather good Christian, and yet he seems to have had little such awareness. We note how the biblical original functions as a critique of inherited presuppositions and incentive to new thought.[21] Few things are more liberating and creative in modern theology than a clear distinction between the "original" and the "translation" in any age, our own included.

21. For a fuller treatment of these issues, see my article "Biblical Theology" in *The Interpreter's Dictionary of the Bible*, vol. 1 (1962), 418–32.

JUDGMENT AND MERCY*

I have been asked to speak on the theme, "Judgment and Mercy," and I have been asked as a theologian. These remarks are thus not to be taken as an antidote to action; rather, they have evolved out of necessity. The need has been evoked by the fact that all of us over these past years have had to reconsider in depth many traditional notions—familiar notions which have sustained us, puzzled us, and irritated us. Theologians often find it useful to juxtapose opposites or correlates such as *judgment* and *mercy*. Our theological vocabularies are well stocked and we think ourselves clever at putting words in pairs, having them balance one another off, sometimes even neutralizing one another. Learned persons have even become accustomed of late to speaking about "dialectic"—a method which can be dangerous because it could be one of those subtle ways in which words neutralize one another, although theologians claim rather that they seek a creative tension between the words. The combination of *judgment and mercy* is one of those pairs which tempt theologians to such a balancing off, to playing one against the other, by dialectic or whatever means.

* Paul's understanding of the Christian life in this world as marked by weakness rather than victory, survival rather than triumph, has—or should have—deep consequences for us all. The upheavals of the late sixties and the sober thinking of the early seventies brought this home to many of us in the United States. To me this line of thinking, feeling, and acting reached a climax at a gathering of civil rights and peace forces at Kansas City, Missouri. At that time, on what happened to be Martin Luther King, Jr. Day, January 15, 1972, I was asked to speak on "Judgment and Mercy." Never has the Pauline model of the theology of the cross struck me as more to the point. This text was never published and I appreciate this opportunity to share the address with a wider audience.

Judgment and mercy is a classical pair of words, pre-Christian, well grounded in the Jewish tradition, not only in the Old Testament but also in the thought of the rabbis and the sages who spoke, for example, about the "two measures," of judgment and of mercy. The rabbis saw these measures as the two hands of God: the hand of mercy was the right hand, the hand of judgment the left. Rabbinic exegesis even attempted to derive from these two attributes of the divine character an explanation of the alternation of the divine names in the Bible, Yahweh (Lord) and Elohim (God). Thus they claimed that wherever Yahweh is used it connotes the attribute of mercy and compassion, and Elohim denotes the divine character of stern and strict judgment. A similar distinction, although in an opposite direction, was attempted by Philo. Since Philo used the Greek translation of the Old Testament, Yahweh was rendered as *kyrios* which suggested the sovereign judging attribute, while Elohim (*theos*) was associated with the gracious merciful attribute of divinity. That such distinctions were not always consistent mattered less than the basic notion of the two measures of the divine character.

In the Christian tradition, judgment and mercy have become engrafted into our spiritual wisdom as we have played the "soul game," transforming practically all of the immense and ferocious drama of history that we read about in the Bible into the kind of pastoral counseling and consolation in which God's mercy overcomes the fear of judgment. That way of plowing such concepts under, and of applying overpowering and majestic words to the intricacies of our little souls has been one of the elements in what Bonhoeffer rightly called "cheap grace," and in what Marx and others rightly recognized as the "opiate of the people."

Such, however, is a totally erroneous way of reading, listening, and understanding the relation between judgment and mercy—at least in respect to the Bible and to Jewish as well as Christian experience. Let me take my point of departure from Isaiah 40, which begins:

Comfort, comfort my people,
   says your God.
Speak tenderly to Jerusalem,
   and cry to her
that her warfare is ended,
   that her iniquity is pardoned,
that she has received from the Lord's hand
   double for all her sins.
A voice cries:
 "In the wilderness prepare the way of the Lord,
   make straight in the desert a highway for our God.
Every valley shall be lifted up,
   and every mountain and hill be made low;
the uneven ground shall become level,
   and the rough places a plain.
And the glory of the Lord shall be revealed,
   and all flesh shall see it together,
   for the mouth of the Lord has spoken."
A voice says, "Cry!"
   And I said, "What shall I cry?"
All flesh is grass,
   and all its beauty is like the flower of the field.
The grass withers, the flower fades,
   when the breath of the Lord blows upon it;
   surely the people is grass.
The grass withers, the flower fades;
   but the word of our God will stand forever.
                                    (Isaiah 40:1–8)

Here is the key to the understanding of judgment and mercy.
To the oppressed, the suppressed, and the repressed, there is no
message with more comfort than to know that "all flesh is
grass" and all the power that lords over them is passing away.
The content of the message of comfort is the downfall of the
"haves," the downfall of the powerful; here there is little or
no comfort at all for the comfortable.   Comfort consists in the
announcement of revolution, of a change of crew, of a leveling

process, of the fact that those who hunger and thirst for justice are finally going to be satisfied.

There is no comfort for the comfortable. Where, then, do the comfortable fit into such a scheme? Where do *we*, most of us, fit into such a scheme? Does this not mean that the kingdom is closer, the will of God more manifest when *we* lose and when things are taken away from *us*? Does this not mean that we actually should not fear such loss? When comfort comes to those who need it, the will of God is made manifest; what could—or, at least, should—be more to our liking? Few are those who are willing to give, but the true believers are those who rejoice when God takes away that which they thought of as theirs, and gives to whomever he wants.

Consider what this means. Judgment and mercy are not balanced over against each other in a scheme in which a last judgment is tempered and adjusted by God's grace, or Christ, or the blood, or the cross, or the intercession of the saints. That is not the way it is. Mercy, salvation, liberation are all part of God's judgment. God's judgment brings mercy to those who need mercy. Judgment is *justice* for those who hunger and thirst after it, those deprived of it. God's judgment is in his activity, when he puts things right, when he establishes justice. It is important to revive and revitalize the biblical meaning of judgment (*krisis*) as that establishment of justice which by necessity means mercy for the wronged and loss for those who have too much.

The English language is a "docetic" language, as we learned theologians say. It has an unusual ability of dividing up words into that which is more spiritual and that which is less spiritual, so that one distinguishes between "justice" and "righteousness." In the world one speaks about justice; and in the church one speaks about righteousness. But in Hebrew, Greek and Latin that escape is not possible. Such a distinction is a peculiarity of languages such as English and German. (In English we even manage to distinguish between Jude, who is good, and Judas, who is evil, although anyone who reads the Bible in the original languages knows that those names are exactly the same. Similarly, English uses the name Jacob in the Old Testament but James in the New, so that it can separate Jews and Christians; but in the original languages, and now many translations, those names are identical.) This phenomenon is worth noting. It is one of those peculiar ways in which language exerts great power over our thought habits and patterns of speech. So also with righteousness and justice: they are the one and only *justitia*.

When God puts things right, the first often become the last and the last the first. That is a glorious amount of mercy—to "the last"—and it is the mercy of which the Bible speaks. Jesus spent little time in convincing the Pharisees that they were at heart sinners. He simply accepted the publicans and the overt sinners, and from that came a change of crew in the operation of the kingdom. The basic point is that we should not think of judgment and mercy as two different aspects in opposition but rather as the *one* thing a believer ponders in his prayer, in his hope, in his reflection, and in his faith. Then comes the question: For whom does the judgment mean mercy and for whom does it mean negative judgment?

In many Christian traditions the theme of the last Sunday in the church year is that of the Last Judgment. In my home church it was even called the Sunday of Doom. In the U.S. it often turns out to be the Sunday after Thanksgiving Day. But that last Sunday after Pentecost, the Sunday before Advent, the Sunday of Christ the King, is the day on which one meditates on the last things, mainly under the image of judgment. In times of trouble that was a bright day of *hope* for the little flock, the oppressed, the suppressed, the repressed. To them there was no other hope than that expressed in an early Christian prayer reported in the *Didache*, a writing from the early second century A.D.: "Let grace come and let this world pass away ... *Marana tha* (Our Lord, come!) Amen."

The same note—sounding something like rejoicing in anarchy—is part of the earliest Christian hope and piety, as is well known from Luke 21:9–28. After a description of the terrible things expected before the final coming of the Kingdom

—wars and rumors of wars, famine, pestilence, internecine strife, persecution, and the greatest distress possible—verse 28 sums it up: "Now when these things begin to take place, look up and raise your heads, because your redemption is drawing near." Judgment is the day eagerly and impatiently awaited, the day of liberation in which God will finally vindicate his faithful ones and establish justice. In spite of this note, however, in the big national churches, increasingly involved with the affairs of state, and increasingly identified with the power of the establishment, it became natural to think and feel, in the style of Amos and other prophets of doom, that the Day of Judgment, the Day of the Lord, is darkness rather than light. Thus, much of Christianity has seen it necessary to seek mercy so as to balance the fear of judgment.

Judgment is the time when God finally brings in the verdict. The question, then, is not how one balances off mercy and judgment, but for whom is judgment mercy and for whom is it threatening doom. For God's people God's judgment is salvation. But who are God's people? Is it not consistently true in the Bible that the only time that language about "God's people" really functions, the only time it is allowed to stand up without the lambasting critique of the prophets, is when it stands for the little ones, the oppressed, the suppressed, the repressed? Is it not true that all language about a chosen people becomes wrong when applied outside the situation of weakness?

In other contexts, this was also Paul's great lesson to the triumphalist and self-assured Christians of his time, to the super-apostles who in his judgment, were overconfident. To them Paul said that for him the Lord's grace was sufficient: ". . . for when I am weak, then I am strong" (2 Cor. 12:9–10). Such an exploding of the concept and image of strength is perhaps the simplest and most overarching message of the life and death of Jesus.

Very interesting changes are always going on in the language of a people (and I apologize for being so centered on language, but as an exegete that is my thing). I refer to the language of a culture and a time and a nation. You may have noticed, as have I, that one of the changes now taking place is that those who are sensitive to the situation today speak less and less about freedom and more and more about liberation. What is the difference? It is the very same difference to which I am pointing in this lecture. Freedom is something that people think they have. Freedom might even be something in the name of which they go out and conquer other people. That has happened, I am told. Freedom is very different from liberation. Liberation as a term is really meaningful either when you do not have freedom or when you have just gained it. Freedom is like manna in the wilderness. It does not keep easily. It spoils quickly. You cannot put it in the refrigerator and call it freedom, because freedom has to be won again and again. And that very insight is better expressed by the word *liberation.*

It is striking to hear Paul say that for freedom Christ has liberated us—and see to it that you carry on the liberation, ". . . stand fast therefore, and do not submit again to a yoke of slavery" (Gal. 5:1). This is not merely to refer to the old discussion about the static and the dynamic. Judgment is the moment in which God liberates—but he can only liberate those who need liberation. Mercy and forgiveness are not merely motifs of gentleness, not a counterforce that softens the blows of God's judgment, a protection, or a kind of asbestos against the heat of judgment. When God's judgment falls, in time and out of time, it *is* mercy to those wronged, and it is doom for those who have done wrong or perpetuated and profited from the wrong of others. Judgment is thus a double edged term—with mercy and vindication, doom and condemnation both held within it.

There is, however, one inch more of mercy, and the Jewish sages knew of it when they spoke about how God's measure of mercy was greater than his measure of negative judgment. There is the great mercy given to us insofar as there is time and chance for repentance, for conversion, for *metanoia*, for turning about to good or turning away from evil. Here is perhaps

the mercy of the gospel: there is still a little time for repentance. That does not seem to be much in the way of mercy,
but it is an enormous amount for those who understand the
situation. In the texts connected with Yom Kippur (the Day
of Atonement), and in the sayings of Jesus in the Sermon on
the Mount, repentance presupposes acts of mending and amend-
ing. "So if you are offering your gift at the altar, and there
remember that your brother has something against you, leave
your gift there before the altar and go; first be reconciled to
your brother, and then come and offer your gift" (Mt. 5:23–
24.). We should note, by the way, that it is not that *you* have
something against your brother—the Westerner tends to read
it that way. The Westerner, perhaps, does not even feel very
guilty before God (whom he encounters in a beautiful I–thou
relationship) if the other person has something against him.
He would say: that is his business. But if he, as a product of
Western culture, has negative feelings toward his brother, he
will feel responsible and anxious to clean it up. Jesus has it
the other way around, in good extrovert fashion: . . . and
(you) remember that your brother or sister has something
against you. That has to be cleaned up first. Repentance
means action in response to the pain of others.

This opportunity for repentance might seem to be a small
thing to all except those who have even the slightest notion of
the magnitude of their sin. Those who have a knowledge of
the evil which they, or their culture, or their country, or their
wealth has caused—the consequences of which are irrevocable
and are fed as poison into the world—they know the meaning
of this mercy, this margin for repentance. Worth considering
is the story about the author of hard-core pornography who
went to church and during the sermon had a genuine conversion
experience. He promised the Lord never again to write pornography, and thus started to write devotional literature
instead. His books of meditations, however, never sold very
well, but his pornography kept on selling. That suggests how
insignificant it is to the world that one little person repents,
because his actions move on. And if that is true about such

trivial things as pornography, how gruesomely true it is about our collective acts, our responsibilities as a nation, and as human beings dirtying up this earth morally and ecologically. If the consequences last, is it really important that the individual or even the people repent? Yes, it is, for them, for God, and perhaps for the future. But the guilt lies heavy.

Mercy is the opportunity for repentance. Protestants are critical of Roman Catholic ideas of penance, not to speak of indulgences. Protestant theology insists that what Christ has done for us is enough. The Swedes say, "It is pathetic to hear mosquitoes cough." And those little penances such as the Hail Marys, pilgrimages, and the like, are, if we consider the magnitude of the drama, like mosquitoes' coughs. But perhaps it is helpful for mosquitoes to cough. The point, however, is that the very awareness that repentance calls for action —and I prefer to speak of reparations rather than pilgrimages —is a lasting and important insight. It is mercy that we are invited to repent and do penance, imaginatively and constructively. God's judgment allows this mercy. It is mercy that *we* are invited to be stripped, as the mercy of justice and liberation comes to those who have been denied both. This is a heavy message for the comfortable—and for those of us who try somehow to sever ourselves from the comfortable even though we cannot. Such knowledge can turn into a nonproductive self-hatred or self-pity; one sometimes understands Cain, "My guilt is heavier than I can bear." And one understands Paul, "You should not be so hard on that man anymore for it might be that he could be swallowed up by his contrition, and that would be to play into the hands of Satan" (2 Cor. 2:5–11).

The mercy which consists in the invitation to repentance includes repentance for things that we did for good reasons. Nobody can come to grips with the drama of history unless he recognizes that most of the evil in this world is done by people who do it for good purposes. Evil is not that popular. If one gathered together a lot of people and said, "Let us be evil together," it would not go over very well. Thanks be to God!

Real evil in this world happens when Satan disguises himself
as an angel of light (2 Cor. 11:14). Real evil in this world
consists in evil being done for good, for humanity, for freedom,
for ideology, or for any of the other pseudo-gods of human life.
That is why the guilt becomes so heavy and has to be unmasked.

Thus the question is not to balance judgment and mercy.
Whenever one reads the Bible or theology, what I would call
the "who-is-who" question always arises. Who speaks to
whom and for whom? The mighty message of God was often
heard in a wrong way because one listened in on the wrong
message. There are many examples of this. Jesus did say,
"Man does not live by bread alone," but he never said that to
a hungry person. When he was faced with hungry persons he
fed them—4000 or 5000. And he massproduced wine in
Cana just to prevent the wedding feast from turning into a
fiasco. It was to Satan that he said, "Man does not live by
bread alone," speaking for and to *himself*. The church, however, often quoted Jesus in the wrong direction—to the hungry, in defense of the well-fed.

Who speaks to whom? For whom is judgment mercy?
That is the question, and unless one understands it, even the
most glorious dialectical understanding of theology becomes
not only counterproductive but evil. Consider the most beautiful of all New Testament messages—the message which must
have been very much in mind, as we gathered here—the message of reconciliation. What a beautiful word! Yet here in
the United States we have been poignantly taught that reconciliation may be a word abused by the comfortable and for the
"haves." Today is Martin Luther King Day, January 15th.
All of us remember well that Thursday evening one April when
the news about his death spread abroad. I remember so
strongly that after only a few minutes, all the networks, inde-
pendently of one another, did what the American media always
do (having learned from Homer presumably that everybody
has to have his standing epithet): they named Martin Luther
King, Jr. "the apostle of nonviolence." All these newscasters,

all of them (whom I saw) white, were ruminating on those glorious words, "apostle of nonviolence," through the night of April 4, 1968. And he was. Of course, it was the *Reverend Dr. Martin Luther King, Jr.*—so one wanted to speak religiously, and in the presence of death it came over well, too. "The apostle of nonviolence" sounded wonderful; it suggested itself. But that was not his message to *us*, the white and comfortable. His message to us was, "Shape up, or else." But to his own, at quite some risk and cost, he was an apostle of nonviolence. That, of course, was much more comforting to us. "Comfort, comfort my people." By using the language of reconciliation, our message sounded congenial, but was self-serving.

That brings us back to where we began. Of course, for him who has and for him who is comfortable, reconciliation is very attractive—the sooner the better, so that we give up as little as possible. That is what reconciliation has come to mean, in stark contrast to the Christian tradition's sign of reconciliation, the cross where Christ gave all in order that reconciliation might be had. Judgment and mercy. We must resist all homogenizing, neutralizing, dialecticizing and balancing acts with these terms. There is little mercy except the chance of repentance for us who sit in judgment; but when judgment comes upon us, there is much mercy for the oppressed. So what shall I cry but the words of Joel, the prophet:

> "Yet even now," says the Lord,
>   "return to me with all your heart,
> with fasting, with weeping, and with mourning;
>   and rend your hearts and not your garments."
> Return to the Lord, your God,
>   for he is gracious and merciful,
> slow to anger, and abounding in steadfast love,
>   and repents of evil . . .
> Blow the trumpet in Zion;
>   sanctify a fast;
> call a solemn assembly;
>   gather the people.

Sanctify the congregation;
   assemble the elders;
gather the children,
   even nursing infants.
Let the bridegroom leave his room,
   and the bride her chamber.
Between the vestibule and the altar
   let the priests, the ministers of the Lord, weep
and say, "Spare thy people, O Lord . . ."
         (Joel 2:12–13, 15–17)

So let *us* weep! And let *them* rejoice when the judgment that comes upon us provides their liberation!

GLOSSOLALIA—
THE NEW TESTAMENT EVIDENCE*

The word *glossolalia* comes into our language from a couple of New Testament references where the Greek expression *glōssais lalein* occurs. The traditional translation "to speak in tongues" is a good one if it is remembered that the English word tongue, like the Greek word *glōssa,* can mean both "tongue" and "language." Paul seems to play on this double meaning in the poetic 1 Corinthians 13, where he has the practice of glossalalia in mind when he opens with the sentence, "If I speak human language or even angelic language, but I do not have love . . ."[1]

I

It is in his grappling with the problems that faced the Corinthian church that Paul happens to give us clear and significant

* This paper was first delivered as part of a conference on the development of the modern charismatic movement sponsored by the Washington Cathedral. In its present form it is taken from the published proceedings of that conference, *The Charismatic Movement,* edited by Michael P. Hamilton (Grand Rapids: Eerdmans, 1975), pp. 49–60, and is reprinted with the permission of the publisher.

1. See below (p. 117) for the differences between Paul's understanding of glossolalia and that found in the Pentecost story (Acts 2:4, 11). The difference is not, however, one between "mere tongues" or "mere sounds" and "languages." The difference is between unintelligible speaking (Paul) and a miraculous communication understood by those who listen (Acts 2). For a dependable introduction to the exegetical questions in the New Testament, see J. Behm, article on *glōssa* in *Theological Dictionary of the New Testament,* ed. Gerhard Kittel (Grand Rapids: Eerdmans, 1964), I, 719–27. Behm's article also gives the relevant material about similar phenomena in surrounding cultures. For a discussion of the "language of angels" in Jewish and early Christian tradition, see Russell P. Spittler, Jr., "The Testament of Job," doctoral thesis, Harvard University, 1971.

insight into the phenomenon of glossolalia as part of the Christian experience. We should perhaps first check our language in one more respect. Scholars and modern readers are quick to put the label "problem" on the topic of glossolalia. And it is obvious that Paul does see problems in the Corinthian church. One of them is the tension created in the congregation by the practices of glossolalia. But it is significant that he does not use that term "problem" when he discusses the glossolalia. To him it is rather the question of gifts, *charismata*, graciously given divine gifts. The genius of his discussion is perhaps exactly in that initial perspective. (As an administrator I have learned that once I have labeled something a problem, then I have already lost the first round.) So we must remind ourselves that we are not dealing with the "problem" of glossolalia, but that we are approaching the subject in a Pauline manner: What about the gift of glossolalia?

We do not get much of a description of glossolalia from Paul or from any other New Testament writer. To Paul it is just an obvious part of the Christian experience, and one with which he is quite familiar from his own practice thereof. We know that Paul has a tendency—an annoying one at that—to claim that he is the greatest in everything. He had been the greatest of sinners, and the hardest of workers for the Gospel, and he had suffered more than all others, etc., etc. So it does not surprise us that when it comes to glossolalia he says, "I thank God that I speak in tongues more than you all" (1 Cor. 14:18). But even if we allow for the arrogant exuberance of Paul, we have reasons to believe him to be a mighty speaker in tongues.

There is other evidence that Paul considered glossolalia to be part of the common Christian experience. I have in mind a passage in his Epistle to the Romans, in which he is not dealing with specific congregational problems that have been brought to his attention. Thus his reference here to glossolalia is not triggered by questions raised about this phenomenon. Paul brings up the subject himself because he thinks it important to remind his readers of this wonderful gift of the Spirit. He says:

> Likewise the Spirit helps us in our weakness; for we do not know how to pray as we ought, but the Spirit itself intercedes with unspeakable groanings; and he who searches the hearts knows what is the mind of the Spirit, for the Spirit intercedes for the saints in a divine manner (or: "according to God's will".) (Rom. 8:26–27)

It is fascinating to notice how Paul comes to think about the role of glossolalia in the context of his argument in Romans 8. He has spoken of how in the cultic cry of "Abba! Father!" the Spirit bears "witness with our spirit that we are children of God" (8:16). He then, in typically Pauline fashion, interrupts the flow of triumphant language and takes great pains to stress how such glories are yet in the future. He speaks of how we groan with the whole of creation as we wait for the redemption to take place. Faith is hope rather than possession. "For who hopes for what he sees?" (8:24). This groaning and beleaguered existence places us in a position of weakness. But now the groaning takes on another connotation. There is an unspeakable sound in the church that is not of human pain and longing but of the Spirit. The unspeakable groan of glossolalia is that of the Spirit interceding for the saints.[2]

Thus, in Paul's mind, the gift of glossolalia is not a sign of spiritual accomplishment, it is not the graduation with high honors into the category of the truly spiritual. To him glossolalia is the gift that fits into his experience of weakness. All this is quite in keeping with Paul's consistent argument against any piety or theology marked by triumphalism, i.e., by an overstatement of spiritual superiority and gnostic flight from the powers of sin and death. It is important to have this

---

2. For a more extensive interpretation of Romans 8:26–27 along these lines, see E. Käsemann, "The Cry for Liberty in the Worship of the Church," *Perspectives on Paul* (Philadelphia: Fortress Press, 1971), pp. 122–37. In his *An die Römer* (Tübingen: J. C. B. Mohr [Paul Siebeck], 1973), pp. 229–32, this interpretation is carefully compared with and defended against other interpretations.

perspective in mind as we turn to his handling of the situation in Corinth.[3]

And so we turn to the Corinthian scene. The church of Corinth had many problems. It had almost all the problems that churches have had through the ages, except the chief problem of our churches today: it was never dull.

It appears that in Corinth the phenomenon of glossolalia had fired the imaginations of the Corinthian Christians. Paul's argument about this and the polarization it created in the congregation is a simple one, built on the image of the body that needs different members (1 Cor. 12). He observes that there are many gifts, all of which are needed, and that it can only be considered silly to play the one gift against the other or to organize them in a hierarchy of value. All these gifts belong to the church and should not be valued or sought on the basis of spectacular appearances.

It is at this point that Paul enters the hymnic plea for love (1 Cor. 13). This familiar passage—often read at weddings for some reason—is not a general praise of love. It is shaped and created for the very specific purpose of demonstrating the solution to the tensions in the Corinthian congregation. The references to glossolalia (13:1, 8), prophecy (13:2, 8), *gnōsis* (i.e., the claim to revealed special knowledge—13:2, 8), the power of miracles (13:2), and the capacity for "helpful deeds" (13:3; cf. 12:28) all point toward the gifts that manifest themselves in the church there. And Paul's point is made obvious when he shows how all these gifts can become divisive unless they are controlled by what he calls love, *agapē*. To him this love is not a feeling in the heart. Love is rather the criterion by which one can distinguish between those on an ego-trip and those who exercise these gifts toward "the build-

---

3. It should be noted that when Paul refers to his having listened to words spoken in Paradise ("and he heard unspeakable words, which are not permissible for humans to speak," 2 Cor. 12:4), he does so as a stress on his own weakness manifested in his "thorn in the flesh," presumably the illness that taught him not to glory in his visions and revelations but in the grace of God (2 Cor. 12:6–10). Compare also 2 Corinthians 4:7 against the preceding words of glorious revelations.

ing up" (*oikodomē*) of the community (1 Cor. 14:4 etc.). In 1 Corinthians 8:1 Paul has given his catchword for this attitude: "*Gnosis* puffs up, but love builds up." And in 1 Corinthians 14 he then proceeds to apply this principle that he has expanded in poetic style in 1 Corinthians 13. It is very clear and simple. The exercise of the gifts of the Spirit should be governed by what best builds up the community. Love means concern for the community and is the check on the exercise of the gifts for personal gratification or the gratification of some rather than all.

From this perspective it makes much sense when Paul, the mighty practitioner of glossolalia, says: "I thank God that I speak in tongues more than you all. Nevertheless, in church I would rather speak five words with my mind, in order to instruct others, than ten thousand words in a tongue" (14:18–19). And if in tongues, then there should also be interpretation (14:27). For "he who speaks in a tongue edifies [builds up] himself, but he who prophesies edifies [builds up] the church" (14:4).

The import of this line of argument could best be expressed by our concluding that to Paul glossolalia is a communication between the believer and God. As such it is a wonderful and treasured gift, part of the complete spectrum of Christian experience. But it is not suited for evangelism or for publicity. It can become divisive when used for any other purpose than the edification of the person who has that gift. It is a family affair, and we may rejoice in the family with those who practice the gift. But with humor and irony he describes at length how singularly nonproductive glossolalia is for those who come into the church as strangers. He says that they will just think you are crazy (14:23).

Now, we know that Paul is not afraid of being a fool for Christ's sake (1 Cor. 4:10). But at this point he is afraid of wrong foolishness. I guess he knew that some Christians love to feel encouraged in their witness by the world's accusing them of being crazy. The more they are labeled crazy the more they feel sure that their witness is strong and courageous.

But did not Paul say that the Greeks seek wisdom and the Jews demand signs, but we preach Christ crucified, a stumbling block to Jews and a folly to Gentiles (1 Cor. 1:22–23)? I think Paul knew how such fearless witness could send him on what we have called ego-trips. At least he sees the risk when others do it, and therefore he brings in his principle of "love," of the building up of the whole community. That "building up" is done better by understandable speaking than by glossolalia. There is a passage in Scripture (Isa. 28:10–11)[4] which uses strange language, words that have no meaning understandable to human beings: sav lasav, sav lasav—kav lakav, kav lakav—zeer sham, zeer sham.[5] Paul quotes God's comment on this to Isaiah: "By strange speakers (*heteroglōssoi*) and by the lips of foreigners shall I speak to this people and even so they will not listen to me" (1 Cor. 14:21).[6]

Interpreters have been thrown by the unexpected shift in Paul's argument at this point. He seems to have been saying that glossolalia is for insiders but that the outsider is lost and cannot say his Amen to a thanksgiving uttered in tongues (1 Cor. 14:16). But now we are told, on the basis of the quote from Isaiah, that glossolalia is for a sign not to believers, but to unbelievers, while prophecy is not for unbelievers but for believers (14:22). After which Paul returns to his plea for the use of prophecy rather than glossolalia in the

4. Paul here uses the term *Law* for a quotation from the prophet Isaiah. This does not indicate that he quotes from memory and remembers wrongly. Jewish practice was to use *Law* for *Scripture*. Cf. Romans 3:19; John 10:34.

5. These words have no meaning. They were meant to be a mimicking either of child talk or of drunken talk or dialect peculiarities of the prophet. But the Septuagint interpreted them as meaning "affliction upon affliction, hope upon hope, yet a little, yet a little"; and the KJV and RSV gave the meaning "precept upon precept, line upon line, here a little there a little." However, Paul was familiar with these words in the Hebrew and untranslatable form. They came to his mind when thinking of glossolalia. Perhaps his reference to childishness and adulthood in 1 Corinthians 14:20 is another indication that he has in mind not only Isaiah 28:11 but the whole passage, since in 28:9 there is a reference to little children.

6. Paul's quotation differs both from the Hebrew text and the Septuagint (although Origen reports that this wording comes close to Aquila). In any case, it is an adapted quotation, serving the point Paul wants to make.

assemblies, and this for the specific reason that prophecy has the power of leading to the conviction and conversion of the outsider.

A resolution of this apparent inconsistency is important for our understanding that according to Paul glossolalia has no function as a means toward impressing the outsiders, that it belongs to the warmth of individual thanksgiving, not to the public realm.

The key to the problem is what Paul means by "sign."[7] I suggest that the word "sign" had a negative connotation for Paul.[8] It refers to a "mere sign," a sign that does not lead to faith but to non-hearing, to the hardening of unbelief. To the believers the glossolalia is not a sign, it is part of their experience. And Paul's point is that the church owes the outsiders and unbelievers who come to the assemblies more than a mere negative sign toward their judgment. It owes them the full opportunity of repentance and the chance to recognize fully that

7. The Greek of 1 Corinthians 14:22 should be translated carefully. The RSV translation, "tongues are a sign not for believers but for unbelievers," overlooks the expression *eis sēmeion* (for a sign). I would translate: "Thus [according to the quotation from Isaiah 28:11] glossolalia becomes [*einai eis*] a (mere) sign not for believers but for unbelievers."

8. In various contexts Paul refers to "signs" where he speaks of matters which for him are wrong (1 Cor. 1:22) or obsolete (circumcision, Rom. 4:11). In 2 Corinthians 12:12 Paul refers to the signs of the true apostle performed among the Corinthians, but it should be noted that this is part of an ironic, tongue-in-cheek exchange about his credentials as compared to other traveling missionaries: "For I am not at all inferior to these super–apostles, even though I am nothing" (12:11). The same expression is echoed in Romans 15:19, where again there is the note of reticence: "For I will not venture to speak . . ." (15:18). In 2 Thessalonians 2:9 the signs are of Satan, and false. In 2 Thessalonians 3:17 Paul's signature is the sign indicating that it is his letter. These (together with 1 Cor. 14:22) are all the references to "signs" in Paul's epistles. None of them refers to signs in a sense or context in which Paul glories unambiguously in them. It is well known that the synoptic Gospels have a similar negative attitude toward signs. In Mark we hear that "no sign will be given" (Mk. 8:12); in Luke the sign is Jonah's preaching (Lk. 11:29); and in Matthew 12:40, possibly by later addition (see K. Stendahl, *The School of St. Matthew*, 2nd ed. [Philadelphia: Fortress Press, 1968], pp. 132f.), the death and resurrection is that sign of Jonah. The miracles of Jesus are never called signs, except in the Gospel of John, where seven chosen miracles are proclaimed and elaborated as "the Signs." Otherwise, signs are celestial and apocalyptic in the cosmic realm. And Jesus' fear of publicity from his miracles is a well-known gospel theme (e.g., Mk. 5:43).

God is truly in the midst of the assembly.   This can be accomplished by prophecy, by the plain and clear speaking of the word of God.[9] It cannot be achieved by glossolalia, which for the outsider simply enforces his alienation, causing him to stumble over the mere sign, as Isaiah had predicted it in that passage.

II

Within the New Testament there is another, and totally different, way of speaking about tongues and about the phenomenon of glossolalia.   In Acts 2 we find an account of the first Christian Pentecost.   It may surprise you that I did not begin there, rather than in Corinth, especially since in this century we have come to use the term *Pentecostals* for groups and churches that give special emphasis to glossolalia.   My reasons for the order I have chosen will soon appear.

In Acts 2 the tongues are tongues as of fire,[10] distributing themselves over the apostles and hovering over them as they,

9. With this interpretation, prophecy is of course not a "sign."   C. K. Barrett, *The First Epistle to the Corinthians* (New York: Harper & Row, 1968), pp. 313, 323f., translates "prophecy as a sign not for the unbelieving . . ."   He admits that "as a sign" is not in the Greek text but must be understood from the preceding sentence.   I submit that there lies the key to the alleged problem with our text.   Thus, I would paraphrase 1 Corinthians 14:21–25 as follows: From the Scriptures we learn that when God speaks through glossolalia, it will not lead to faith [*eisakousontai*: they will not hear, a prophetic future used by Paul to refer to the situation now at hand in the church].   Thus it is clear, according to this prophetic word, that glossolalia is a mere sign, incapable of leading the unbeliever to faith.   Of course, to the believer glossolalia is not such a sign, for he has listened to the word of God and come to faith.   Prophecy, on the other hand, is toward faith and not toward the hardening of unbelief.   Thus, if in the assembly all speak with tongues, and outsiders and nonbelievers come in, will they not just say that you are mad?   The sign of glossolalia will work on them as Isaiah has predicted.   But if all speak in understandable prophecy, then the nonbeliever or the outsider will be brought to repentance, convicted and judged as the secrets of his heart are laid open and he falls down, worshiping God and declaring that God is really among you.

10. Note Mark 1:8, Matthew 3:11, and Luke 3:16, where John the Baptist makes the distinction between his baptism (by water) and that of the Greater One to come, who will baptize in the Holy Spirit (Mark) or in the Holy Spirit and fire (Matthew and Luke).

full of the Spirit, begin to speak in "other tongues" (*heterai glōssai*). This happens in Jerusalem, accompanied by the sound of a mighty wind from heaven. It appears that here the situation is the opposite of that in Corinth: This glossolalia is not in need of interpreters. The speaking with tongues is a miraculous and marvelous means of communication so that a large number of people from diverse countries hear in their own tongues the disciples proclaim "the mighty works of God" (2:11). It seems that the tragic breakdown in communication at the Tower of Babel (Gen. 11:6–9) has been overcome. This contrast to the understanding of glossolalia that emerges from Paul's discussion in 1 Corinthians is striking, and it is not obviated or softened by the various discussions about whether the miracle in Acts 2 is one of speaking (the apostles speaking different languages or dialects), or one of hearing (the listeners recognizing a "heavenly" language as their own true language).[11] In either case the difference remains between intelligible (Acts) and unintelligible (Paul) glossolalia.[12] I am, however, inclined to think that little is to be gained by this

11. For extensive discussion of these and other exegetical questions, see Kirsopp Lake, "The Gift of the Spirit and the Day of Pentecost," *The Beginnings of Christianity*, eds. F. J. Foakes-Jackson and Kirsopp Lake (London: MacMillan, 1933), V, 111–21; see also E. Haenchen, *The Acts of the Apostles* (Philadelphia: Westminster Press, 1971), pp. 166–75.

12. I fail to see the validity of C. S. C. Williams' assertion in *A Commentary on the Acts of the Apostles* (New York: Harper & Brothers, 1957), p. 63, that "those who adopt the ordinary critical view tend to overlook that even to Paul glossolalia may well have meant or included speaking in foreign tongues, as well as unintelligible speech, not the latter alone." He refers to J. G. Davies, "Pentecost and Glossolalia," *Journal of Theological Studies*, III (1952), 228–31. Davies argues that the term *hermeneia/hermeneuein*, which Paul uses for the interpretation of glossolalia (1 Cor. 12:10, 30; 14:5, 13, 26, 27) has the primary meaning of "translate" rather than "interpret." That is correct, and obviously Paul thought about glossolalia as a language, even as the language of angels (1 Cor. 13:1). But that does not mean that he understood it as the acquisition of knowledge of an earthly foreign language. Tongues are unintelligible, since they express "mysteries in the Spirit" (1 Cor. 14:2). And Paul urges the speaker of tongues to "pray that he be able also to interpret" (14:13). It is not by knowing other languages, but by the special gift of interpretation/translation, that these mysteries can be made intelligible to others.

line of reasoning. We must rather begin by considering the nature of the Pentecost account and its function within that work called the Acts of the Apostles.

The account of Pentecost is unique in the sense that nowhere else in the New Testament or in the early extra-canonical literature is there ever a reference to such an event. While we have practically no Christian literature that does not hail the event of Easter, there is no reference to Pentecost as an event except in Acts. All Christian literature is aware of the Spirit being around. But the account of a specific event rests solely on the author of the Book of Acts. It may well be that he, the author, is the one who has stylized and put into story form a theological interpretation of the phenomenon of speaking with tongues. Furthermore, nowhere else in early Christian literature is there any understanding of glossolalia as the speaking of a language known in some other part of the world. The very point of glossolalia elsewhere in early Christian tradition is that it needs an interpreter, that it is unintelligible; i.e., that it is just as described in the Corinthian correspondence. But in Acts it sounds as if there were a divine shortcut to the Berlitz school. It is also questionable whether the places from which the hearers come (Acts 2:9–11) really represent distinct languages.

It must be recognized that the very structure of the Book of Acts is one of "theological geography." Just as in the Gospel of Luke Jesus moves from Galilee to Jerusalem—and much of the narrative and teaching is comprised in the so-called Lukan Travel Narrative (Lk. 9:51–18:14); this in complete variance with the other gospels—so in Acts the Gospel is brought from Jerusalem (ch. 1) to Rome (ch. 28), and the scheme is announced in the parting words of the Risen Lord prior to his ascension, when he promises the coming of the Spirit as the starting point for such a mission out of Jerusalem "to the end of the earth" (Acts 1:8).

Thus it is tempting to follow the rather common suggestion that Luke has translated his awareness of how the Spirit is abroad in the church and his acquaintance with the phenomenon of glossolalia into a historic event, of which we have no other evidence. The global outreach is symbolized by the phenomenon of glossolalia.[13] If this is true, then it becomes rather precarious—to say the least—to base our understanding of the actual phenomenon of glossolalia on the account in Acts 2.[14]

III

In our discussion of the Pauline attitude toward glossolalia and the spectacular gifts of the Spirit we had reason to stress quite strongly how such gifts were not to operate in the public domain. Actually, it is worth asking how the early Christians thought of their relation to the public world, and, more especially, how and where they saw the point of intersection between the church and the world. The reason for my raising that question within a study of glossolalia is perhaps less obvious. Yet the connection is an important one.

We have said that the spectacular gifts of the Spirit are for

13. Such a suggestion is partly confirmed by the observation that when glossolalia is mentioned at other points in Acts (10:46; 19:6; cf. 4:31), the phenomenon appears much more similar to the picture we receive in 1 Corinthians 12—14. In Acts 10, for example, there is no reference to language difficulties. Rather, the point is that God has to overcome Peter's hesitations concerning Gentile membership in the church by having Cornelius and his people show the spectacular evidence of the Spirit, all of which led Peter to declare that there could be no reason not to baptize those who had received the Holy Spirit "just as we have" (Acts 10:47). Here the Spirit—manifested by glossolalia— does not cross linguistic or geographical barriers, but the barrier between Jews and Gentiles.

14. Our traditional Bibles include one further passage in which the Christian mission is pictured as including the speaking of "new tongues" (Mk. 16:17). As can now be seen in the RSV, NEB, and other modern editions of the Bible, verses 9–20 of Mark 16 were not part of the original text and are missing in the most dependable of the ancient manuscripts. Nevertheless, the text in "Mark 16:17" could be taken as evidence for how the understanding expressed in Acts 2 caught the imagination of the church, especially when the topic was the missionary outreach, i.e., the very topic of "Mark 16:9–20." Note, however, that some manuscripts do not read "new tongues" but "tongues," thus referring rather to the general phenomenon of glossolalia.

the edification of the individual and not for public relations. But a special gift of the Spirit *is* promised for the most public of relations in which a Christian could be involved: "And when they bring you to trial and deliver you up (to the authorities), do not be anxious beforehand what you are to say; but say whatever is given to you in that hour, for it is not you who speak, but the Holy Spirit" (Mk. 13:11; see also Mt. 10:19–20, Lk. 12:11–12). As a matter of fact, the Christian before the courts is the only one to whom the Scriptures promise the gift of the Spirit. No one individual is otherwise promised a special gift of the Spirit. This is not so strange, for it was in the courts that the Christian church had the opportunity to witness to the powers of this world. Out of this view and conviction comes the elaborate account of how Paul appealed to Caesar although he presumably could have been freed (Acts 25:11; 26:32), and also the passage in Ephesians (3:10–13) in which appearing before Caesar and confronting the heavenly principalities and powers blend into one, and in which Paul's sufferings are the glory of the church, since the judicial process occasions the confrontation between the Gospel and the world, between Christ and Caesar. To be a witness (the Greek word is "martyr") is to be a witness before the authorities. Thus there should be no surprise when we find that the Spirit is especially promised for such a situation.

This line of biblical thinking strikes me as significant at this time. The concern for the gifts of the Spirit in the charismatic movement has sometimes been seen as being at the opposite end of the spectrum from the exposed place where we find the Berrigans and the conscientious resisters in our land. If that feeling and interpretation were correct (and it is often enforced by the press and the other media), then we are seriously removed from a biblical understanding of the gifts of the Spirit. Then we have distorted deep Christian insight. There are those who identify the public impact of the Spirit with spectacular religious exhibitions on TV and maximum publicity for evangelistic campaigns, while casting suspicion over those who challenge the authorities by their courageous witness to Christ's justice in the courts. It seems that the biblical model is the opposite one. In the courts is *the* confrontation that has the promise of the Spirit.

IV

It seems to me that the witness of the New Testament texts as to the phenomenon called glossolalia is quite clear and quite simple—and quite up to date. The various texts carry with them a certain critique of the situation today. The history of our main traditions is one of fragmentation and impoverishment within the Christian community. As I read Paul it seems to me crystal clear that if the Presbyterians and the Episcopalians, the Lutherans, and all the "proper" Christians, including the Catholics, did not consciously or unconsciously suppress such phenomena as glossolalia, and if other denominations did not especially encourage them, then the gifts of the Spirit—including glossolalia—would belong to the common register of Christian experience.

The Pauline recipe is sound. The fullness of the church cannot be better ridiculed than by the habit, long established, according to which every denomination or sect takes its gift of the Spirit and builds a special little chapel around it. The fullness of the church is, in the image of Paul, the body of Christ with many and diverse members, i.e., gifts.

There are signs at this time in the charismatic movement that we may have the chance to restore that fullness. And that is what fascinates me and gives me much hope in the charismatic movement. Could it be that we have come to a time when the main line churches have enough Pauline love so as to be ready to accept within them the manifestations of the Spirit, including glossolalia? Could it be that those blessed with this experience could have enough love and patience as they speak to the Lord in the Spirit so as to recognize that they were given that gift in order to add to the fullness of the church, not in order to make others feel less Christian in their faith? Perhaps we are at that point. I hope we are, and that for the benefit of us all.

Glossolalia is a facet of what I like to see as high-voltage religion. It is obvious to me that to some people, and in some situations, the experience of God is so overwhelming that charismatic phenomena are the "natural" expression. In the history of religions and of the church there is an honorable place for ecstasy. Who said that only rational words or silence would be proper? As a preacher and lecturer, I even wonder if it is not wise to let glossolalia gush forth in the church so that those who are not professional in the shaping of words are free to express fully their overwhelmed praise to the Lord. Actually, in the history of the church the practice of glossolalia has often had a democratizing effect. It has been one of the expressions through which in a certain sense "the last have become the first."

Opening up the full spectrum of religious experience and expression is badly needed in those churches that have suppressed the charismatic dimension. Flashlight-battery-voltage Christianity is certainly not strong enough for fighting the drug habit. And no religious tradition can renew itself without the infusion of raw and fresh primary religious experience. It could well be that the charismatic movement is given to the churches as one such infusion. We noncharismatics need not become charismatics—glossolalia is a gift, not a goal or an ideal—but we need to have charismatics among us in the church if the church is to receive and express the fullness of the Christian life. Thus *we* need *them*.

Those churches that have suppressed charismatic manifestations often argue that the biblical phenomenon of glossolalia was given to the early church for its breakthrough period, that once the church was established, such "primitive" things were no longer needed. Such reasoning has a defensive ring. The defensiveness is one of embarrassment, either for the absence of what the Bible describes as part of the full Christian experience, or for what "enlightened" Christians perceive as unsavory and primitive in the annals of their tradition.

When used in such a setting, the idea of a breakthrough period does not commend itself. But there is another sense in which it has meaning and contains wisdom born out of experience. For it seems to me that few human beings can live healthily with high-voltage religious experience over a long period of time. While I reject the breakthrough argument on the plane of institutional history, I am very sympathetic to it when applied to individual history. I am concerned about what happens to charismatics after five or ten or twenty years. From my observations it seems that *they* need *us*; they need to know that their home is the larger church in which their status as children of God does not depend on the intensity of their experiences. There are times and seasons in the long life of a Christian. There are times of spectacular breakthroughs and there are times of slow growth. Understandably, those who have had strong and beautiful experiences like to have them continue. If that experience eventually does not come quite as freshly and as strongly as it once did, then comes the temptation to "help the Spirit" a little—that is, to cheat. Which creates feelings of guilt. To be sure, the established churches need the refreshing influx of new and wider ranges of charismatic experience, but in the long perspective of spiritual growth the individual charismatic needs the home of the full church in which he or she matures in faith and learns the most important lesson of faith: to love God who gave the gift rather than to love the gift that God gave. That lesson can be learned only in a church where we rejoice with the charismatics in the gifts given to them—they are the precious seasoning of our common life—and where those who are given such gifts can grow in faith without feeling threatened if their experiences change during a long and honest life.

These reflections grow out of Paul's insights into the fullness of the church and the building up of our common life. They are born out of the conviction that the question of glossolalia in the churches is a pastoral one. It is not a question of whether glossolalia is a theologically proper phenomenon—of course it is. It is rather a question of how this phenomenon can be a force to the benefit of the whole church. It is in that sense that Paul's vision and perspective strike me as unsurpassed both in wisdom and validity.

It may prove important to pursue further how glossolalia is an integral part of what all religions know as mysticism, and how it relates to the practices and experiences of Christian mystics. I am inclined to think that such an analysis would reinforce the criterion mentioned above: not the gift that God gave, but God who gave the gift. The charismatics are in danger of becoming fascinated by the gift. The mystics are the pioneers in transcending all gifts so as never to rest until God is All in All. Which is another reason for saying that we need to stay together in that love which allows a maximum of diversification in gifts as God gives them differently and at different times.

SOURCES AND CRITIQUES

No theologian operates in a vacuum. My own work has been shaped by overarching concerns, and it might be helpful to the reader if I shared my own understanding of them. They are basically two.

1) The principles of biblical interpretation, or what the learned community calls *hermeneutics* (I would prefer to use the expression, "how the church lives with its Bible"). The longer I work as an exegete, the more serious becomes the question of the uses and misuses of Scripture. The responsibility of interpretation is a grave one, and these essays are an attempt at minimizing the risks of misuse, thus setting the texts free for peaceful, liberating, and salvific use. I believe that the *first* and indispensable step in any such enterprise is to insist on a clear distinction between what a text *meant* according to its original intention, and what it came to mean and/or might mean at any later point in history or the future. For such a hermeneutical program, see my article on "Biblical Theology, Contemporary" in *Interpreter's Dictionary of the Bible*, Vol. I, 418–32 (Nashville: Abingdon Press, 1962). Such a program requires us never to ask "What does it mean?" without adding ". . . to whom?"

I became especially aware of this issue in my essay, *The Bible and the Role of Women* (Philadelphia: Fortress Press, 1966), and even more so when I came to the conclusion that Paul's words in Romans 12:20 about "collecting fire on your enemies' head" are almost as gruesome as they sound (see "Hate, Non-Retaliation and Love," *Harvard Theological Review* 55 [1962], 343–55). That strange sentiment also possesses a religious and ethical value when seen as an expression of non-retaliation—not pursuing one's own vengeance. The question is, as always, "Who speaks for whom?" as described in the third essay of this book, "Judgement and Mercy." To Paul —to Luther—and by the help of the Spirit, to us . . .

This concern requires serious attention to the fact that the biblical writings function as Scripture in the Christian tradition. Hence these essays give attention from time to time to the question of Canon. The article by Albert C. Sundberg, Jr., "Canon Muratori: A Fourth Century List," (*Harvard Theological Review* 66 [1973], 1–41) has been of importance to me. On Scripture as a phenomenon and how to cope with its power, it is instructive to study W. C. Smith, "The Study of the Bible" (*Journal of the American Academy of Religion* 39 [1971], 131–40).

2) The other concern that has grown out of my studies of Paul, increasingly catching my fascination and becoming an unexpected priority in my life and work, is that of the relations between Judaism and Christianity, or more correctly expressed, between the church and the Jewish people. What began as a scholarly and intellectual curiosity led me to recognize how the Christian use of Scripture, and not least of the Pauline epistles, had caused developments of satanic dimensions. The first two essays in this book are partly an attempt to get at some of the roots of Christian anti-Semitism. It might be useful to list here some of my further studies which deal more specifically with these questions:

"Judaism and Christianity," *Harvard Divinity Bulletin* [1963]; reprinted in Martin Marty and D. G. Peen (eds.), *New Theology No. 2* (New York: Macmillan and Co., 1965), 153–64.

"Judaism and Christianity II: After a Colloquium and a War," *Harvard Divinity Bulletin* [1967]· most recently reprinted in Frank E. Talmage (ed.), *Disputad Dialogue: Readings in the Jewish-Christian Encounter* (New York: KTAV, 1975), 330–42.

"Towards World Community" in *Jewish-Christian Dia-*

logue: Six Years of Christian-Jewish Consultations, published by the International Jewish Committee on Interre-
ligious Consultations and the World Council of Churches'
agency on Dialogue with Peoples of Living Faiths and
Ideologies (1975).
"In No Other Name," in *Christian Witness and the
Jewish People* (Geneva: Lutheran World Federation,
1976).

When the first two essays in this book assert that Paul's
argument about justification by faith neither grows out of his
"dissatisfaction" with Judaism, nor is intended as a frontal
attack on "legalism," I believe that I am striking at the most
vicious root of theological anti-Judaism. In my discussion
with Ernst Käsemann (see below, pp. 129 ff) I shall elaborate
on this claim.

These essays work from the presupposition that only some
of the Letters of Paul were actually written/dictated/signed
(see Gal. 6:11) by him. They are 1 Thessalonians, Galatians,
1 and 2 Corinthians, Philippians, Philemon, and Romans. I
agree with Günther Bornkamm's position on these questions in
his *Paul* (New York: Harper & Row, 1971 [German original:
1969], pp. 241–43). In other respects, too, I find Bornkamm's
book the best available general introduction to Paul. I refer
primarily to Part I, on Paul's "Life and Work," and especially
to his treatment of "Romans as Paul's Testament" (pp. 88–
96) which stresses how Romans must be interpreted in the light
of Paul's ministry and not on the basis of guesses about con-
flicts among Christians in Rome. Here Bornkamm is at the
opposite end of the scholarly spectrum from the recent attempt
by Paul S. Minear, *The Obedience of Faith,* Studies in Biblical
Theology II:19 (London and Naperville: SCM Press and Alec
R. Allenson, 1971), who has painted an intricate picture of
how Paul speaks to the conditions of the Christians in Rome.
Such reconstructions usually fall back on the late secondary
and inconclusive information in "Ambrosiaster." In spite of
my appreciation of Bornkamm's work, I shall, however, point
out how his picture of Paul and Judaism suffers from a com-

mon "western" flaw (see below, pp. 132–33), a flaw that should
be kept in mind when one makes use of the second part of his
Paul, "Gospel and Theology."

If I were to answer a question as to which more recent
works on Paul have contributed most to whatever new insights
and perspectives are mine, I would mention without hestitation
the works of Dieter Georgi—unfortunately not yet translated
into English. He has placed Paul into a rich context of Hellenistic culture—Jewish and Gentile—in such a fashion as to
dissolve the increasingly fruitless debate between those who
see Paul primarily in the light of his "Jewish background'" and
those who see him primarily in the context of Gentile Hellenistic culture, religion, and popular philosophy. The dissolu-
tion of the Jewish/Hellenistic dichotomy of New Testament
scholarship dawned upon me—outside the area of Pauline
studies—when I prepared an updated introduction for the
second edition of my book, *The School of St. Matthew* (Philadelphia: Fortress Press, 1968, pp. i–xiv). It must have come
as a surprise and even as a shock to some of my colleagues of
"Jewish background" that the author of that book, a detailed
Qumran-like study of Matthew, now saw the Matthean Gospel
as a "Hellenistic" phenomenon and as belonging to a predominantly Gentile community. In that preface I have argued in
a way which helps explain the view of Matthew offered in this
present volume.

The work of Professor Georgi on "the collection" is a blue-
print of Paul's place in the total spectrum of early Christianity.
Georgi's major works are: *Die Gegner des Paulus im 2. Korin-
therbrief: Studien zur religiösen Propaganda in der Spätantike*
["Paul's Opponents in 2 Corinthians: Studies in the Religious
Propaganda of Late Antiquity"] (Neukirchen/Vluyn: Neukir-
chener Verlag, 1964) and *Die Geschichte der Kollekte des
Paulus für Jerusalem* ["The History of Paul's Collection for
Jerusalem"] (Hamburg: Herbert Reich Er. Verlag, 1965). In
English his chapter on how the Hellenistic world perceived
Paul, "Paul from the Greek Side" will appear in the *Cambridge
History of Judaism*, Vol. 2 (expected in 1977), and he is pre-

paring a major commentary on 2 Corinthians to appear in the *Hermeneia* series (Philadelphia: Fortress Press).

Just as the 1950's were marked by the great impetus given to scholarship by the Dead Sea Scrolls—which gave welcome control over various hypotheses about first century Palestinian Judaism—we are now reaping the fruits of the Coptic Gnostic library at Nag Hammadi. These fruits allow both an enrichment of and even better control over Pauline interpretation. Elaine Hiesey Pagels has furnished the readers of Paul's letters with a convenient tool in *The Gnostic Paul* (Philadelphia: Fortress Press, 1975). She provides various Gnostic interpretations, letter by letter and chapter by chapter, of the Pauline material. A whole world and line of interpretation, with its sources at the very beginning of the Christian movement, comes alive. Her work teaches us that whatever Paul's intentions might have been, his writings were capable of being transposed into powerful systems of Gnostic speculation. To me this is a mighty warning against "deeper" interpretations, standing in opposition to the temptation always facing religious persons to honor Paul and God by adding "depth" to the words and the Word. Paul wrote and spoke, we must remember, with humility.

Ernst Käsemann has written an extensive critique of my article on "Paul and the Introspective Conscience of the West" (*Perspectives on Paul* [Philadelphia: Fortress Press, 1971] pp. 60–78 [German original: 1969]). I should like now to respond to that serious critique. At this point it is appropriate, too, to mention with awe and admiration his more recent commentary on Romans, *An die Römer* (Tübingen: J. C. B. Mohr [Paul Siebeck], 1974; English translation soon to appear). This magisterial work will for a long time remain a milestone in the study of Romans—filled as it is with rich insights and written with passionate conviction about the rightness and urgent actuality of a Protestant view of Paul. It is a great honor for me to enter into debate with this master of Protestant exegesis.

Käsemann sees my line of thinking as a serious threat to
Protestantism—which for him means a threat to an authentic
understanding of both Paul and Jesus. I share with him a deep
concern for the theological consequences of exegetical work,
but I am not sure that "the gospel" can be so easily summarized
under the rubric of "the justification of the ungodly" (Rom.
4:5, cf. 5:6; Käsemann, p. 75, 78 *et passim*)—or, for that
matter, in any other single theme, Pauline or not. Similarly, I
am not convinced that the insights of the Reformation depend
on perpetuating such an interpretation of Paul as Käsemann
champions.

I am, however, primarily struck by the manner in which
Käsemann summarizes what he calls "the Stendahl thesis":
"the introspective attitude of the West has led to a false stress
on Paul's struggle with the Judaistic interpretation of the
law and hence to an equally wrong emphasis on the doctrine
of justification which grew out of that struggle" (p. 60). And
he intimates (pp. 70, 71) that I consider the doctrine of justification "a fighting doctrine, directed against Judaism," a view
that he holds dear.

If my article was that misleading, and if the matter is not
sufficiently clarified in this book, allow me to state what is,
and what I thought was, my "thesis." Paul's arguments concerning justification by faith have *not* grown out of his "struggle with the Judaistic interpretation of the law," and are *not*
"a fighting doctrine, directed against Judaism." Its place and
function, especially in Romans, are not primarily polemic, but
apologetic as he defends the right of Gentile converts to be full
members of the people of God. When he uses the argument
"justification by faith" in Galatians, he defends the rights of
his Gentile converts against the practice of "Judaizing," i.e., of
Gentiles submitting to circumsion and food laws. Furthermore, there is no basis for believing that Paul had any *personal*
difficulties in obeying the law.

This "thesis" of mine is thus both more radical than Käsemann recognizes, and more specific in its exegetical argument
than he seems to allow. It is a pity that he chooses to confine
his discussion to Romans, since a significant part of my ques-

tioning of the tradition is based on the observation that Paul's idea of justification does not permeate his writings—and hence is ill suited to be the key to his theology.

This being so, I find it difficult to answer Käsemann. Instead of showing that my exegetical observations are wrong, he chooses to construct a dichotomy in which I have placed "salvation history thematically over against the doctrine of justification" (p. 66). His article thus proceeds to deal with all the evils in the church and the world that can and have come from "theologies of history," including naive cultural optimism and abhorrent Nazism (p. 64). Similarly, I could list how pogroms and the Holocaust found fuel and comfort in an understanding of Judaism as the eternally condemned and evil way to serve God, in the notion that the Jews (including Qumran) suppose the "justification of the godly" to be the aim of the divine plan (cf. Käsemann, p. 75), the same Jews who in A.D. 70 "buried their eschatological hopes in its (the Temple's) ruins" (p. 74), and this, according to Käsemann, because they had a wrong theology of history.

But the first issue at hand is whether Paul intended *his* argument about justification to answer the question: How am I, Paul, to understand the place in the plan of God of my mission to the Gentiles, and how am I to defend the rights of the Gentiles to participation in God's promises? *or*, if he intended it to answer the question, which I consider later and western: How am I to find a gracious God? That is an exegetical question which I have tried to answer—and which can doubtlessly be dealt with differently.

If it is these alternatives that Käsemann refers to by "setting sa vatı history over against the doctrine of justification," then he seem to beg the question by taking the term justification by faith in the traditional Protestant sense, and doing this in a debate where that traditional interpretation of Paul is the precise question at issue. I am suggesting that in Paul the very argument about justification by faith functions within his reflection on God's plan for the world. I may be wrong, but I surely have no special interest in defending abstract propositions about theologies of history.

Käsemann suggests that my line of thinking leads with inner necessity to triumphalism. As a Lutheran theologian, and as a twentieth century Westerner, I am as concerned as he with the evils of triumphalism, and this present book should make that clear. Even in 1963 my article in question stated—though briefly—that the Pauline basis for anti-triumphalism is not to be sought in his teaching about justification, but partly in his emphasis on "weakness," and partly in the eschatological accent on our still groaning with the creation—however one interprets the relation between the two. In neither case is justification by faith at issue.

I would now add that one of the most striking elements of Pauline anti-triumphalism lies exactly in the fact that in Romans Paul does not fight Judaism, but reaches a point where he warns the Gentile Christians against feelings of superiority toward Judaism and the Jews (Rom. 9–11, esp. 11:11–35 which climaxes in a non-christological doxology). When it dawns on Paul that the Jesus movement is to be a Gentile movement—God being allowed to establish Israel in his own time and way—then we have no triumphalist doctrine, but a line of thought which Paul uses in order to break the religious imperialism of Christianity. I also read this as a profound warning against that kind of theological imperialism which triumphs in its doctrine of the justification of the ungodly by making Judaism a code word for all wrong attitudes toward God.

For somewhat similar reasons I part ways with Günther Bornkamm's final paragraphs in his discussion of Romans in *Paul*. Bornkamm has seen clearly that the issue in Romans and especially in chapters 9–11 is not the Judaizers or "this or that section in a particular church, but the Jews." But he interprets these Jews as Paul's opponents and thus reads Romans as "throughout polemical" against "the Jews and their understanding of salvation." I would again stress that Paul is not carrying out such a polemic against the Jews, but is rather giving an apology for his mission in which he reflects on the mystery of God's dealings with Israel.

Even more important to me, however, is it to point out how for Bornkamm this polemic widens by the traditional device of saying: "In a way the Jew symbolizes man in his highest potentialities; he represents the 'religious man' whom the Law tells what God requires of him, who appeals to the special statute granted him in the plan of salvation, and who refuses to admit that he has failed to measure up to God's claim on him and is in consequence abandoned to sin and death." This may serve as a classical picture of that understanding of Paul and Judaism which I have come increasingly to question. It is an unwarranted, freehand drawing of Judaism, impossible to substantiate in Jewish texts. On this matter, see Charlotte Klein, *Theologie und Anti-Judaismus* (München: Chr. Kaiser Verlag, 1975 and published in English in 1978 by Fortress Press, Philadelphia, and SPCK, London) who clearly describes and analyzes how the view of Judaism prevalent in continental New Testament studies has influenced theology.

It could be argued, of course, that the manner typified by Bornkamm is how Paul saw Judaism—which I doubt. Actually, this present book was written in order to substantiate that doubt, and sketch some alternatives. In any case, the first question to raise is whether such a use of justification by faith is an authentic or even a legitimate use of Pauline thinking.